The Complete Resume Guide

The Complete Resume Guide

by MARIAN FAUX

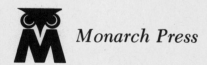 *Monarch Press*

Copyright © 1980 by Marian G. Faux
All rights reserved
including the right of reproduction
in whole or in part in any form.
Published by Monarch Press
A Simon & Schuster Division of
Gulf & Western Corporation
Simon & Schuster Building
1230 Avenue of the Americas
New York, New York 10020

MONARCH PRESS and colophon are trademarks
of Simon & Schuster, registered in the
U.S. Patent and Trademark Office.

Designed by Irving Perkins
Manufactured in the United States of America
10 9 8 7 6 5 4 3 2

Library of Congress Cataloging in Publication Data

Faux, Marian G.
  The complete resume guide.

  Bibliography: p.
  I. Resumes (Employment) I. Title.
HF5383.F34   650'.14   79-12208
ISBN 0-671-18393-1

Contents

HOW TO USE THIS BOOK

This book has two purposes. First, it is meant to explain and discuss with you how you can use your resume to sell yourself. What belongs in a resume—and more important, what has no place in a resume—is discussed in detail.

Second, this book is intended to be a sourcebook as well as a permanent record for you. Several chapters are devoted to forms that will help you know yourself and your career objectives better. Other chapters contain forms that will become a dossier on yourself—information kept readily at hand that can be pulled out any time you need to revise your resume or perhaps consider new job directions and possibilities. In this sense, this book is meant to serve as a sourcebook.

Several chapters discuss the problems resume writers confront—and what to do about them.

A large section is devoted to sample resumes. While it obviously will not be possible for you to copy a resume from this book—your life is too individual for that—looking at what other persons have written will enable you to glean ideas and suggestions for your own resume. Plan to study these resumes carefully not only for what they say and how they say it but also for how they look, an important facet of resume writing that is considered in a special chapter of this book.

ACKNOWLEDGMENTS

Special thanks go to my typist, Judy Waggoner.

A measure of gratitude also goes to the numerous persons who talked with me about resume writing and who generously offered their own resumes as samples for this book.

I am perhaps most indebted to the Forty Plus Club of New York, a group of unemployed executives who help themselves find new positions. They gave graciously of their time and advice, and their advice was excellent.

Introduction

Resumes are the hallmark of the capable, professional worker. They show off your intelligence, your organizational and thinking skills, and your ability to sell yourself.

A resume is first of all a selling tool. Its purpose is to sell you. The preparation of a resume, therefore, is no light matter. It requires days of thought, preparation, and actual writing.

Who needs a resume? Anyone who seeks to impress a prospective employer with his or her skills. Secretaries need them. Plant foremen need them. Paralegals and lawyers need them. Teachers need them. Even persons who may not think they need them or who have never used them before may find that a resume is an innovative way to get a step ahead of the competition.

Every year more and more businesses require resumes, and resumes have become an effective way of pre-screening applicants for jobs.

Surprisingly, even seemingly sophisticated workers often do not know how to write an effective resume. Some persons stubbornly stick to old rules for resume writing that they learned in high school; others fail to promote themselves as much as they might.

Writing a resume is important business. Done properly, it is a key tool in helping you get the job you want. Done improperly, it may leave you wondering why you are so often passed over for jobs without even an interview. Resumes are an important tactic in setting up interviews.

Writing an outstanding resume is one of the rituals of the business world that is well worth mastering.

THE CONTENT OF A RESUME

Once you have determined what kind of job you want, you can begin to think about what goes into your resume. Resumes are highly personal and individual. They vary with the kind of job you are seeking. If you are an engineer or a home economist, or have had several years of work experience, you may find yourself with several possible directions to go in search of a job. These directions may require preparing not one but several resumes, each geared to a specific category of job. Then, too, you may have an opportunity to go for a very special kind of job, and you will want to write a resume especially for that. The more skilled you are, the greater the chance that you will need two or more resumes to meet your job-hunting needs. Fortunately, once a basic resume has been prepared, as well as a file of information on yourself that you can constantly update, spin-off resumes are fairly simple to prepare.

Your Resume as a Selling Tool

The single most important function of your resume is to sell you. In many instances, your resume will arrive at a prospective employer's door before you do. It will determine in large part whether you get an interview for the job you are seeking.

Even if you have met a prospective employer at a party or some other event and engaged him in a conversation that led to a request for your resume, a poorly done resume can blow the possibility of a job. So it is all too easy to imagine how quickly you can lose in the resume game if you send a poorly done resume to someone who has never even laid eyes on you.

How do you write a resume that presents you in your best light? First, it must be well-organized. It must look good and be graphi-

1

cally pleasing to the eye. It must contain all the necessary information about you. It must sell you as a serious job candidate with many qualifications and skills to offer an employer.

A Well-Organized Resume   A resume must be well-organized. This not only means that what you write must be carefully thought out but also that the overall design and format must be pleasing to the eye and logically arranged on the page. Chapter 2 goes into detail about the physical appearance of your resume and how to plan it. Chapters 4 and 5 will help you cull information about yourself and then actually write a resume that describes you and shows you off.

These combined elements should produce a well-organized resume that shows you have organizational skills—and a person who can condense a lifetime's worth of work and education into one to three pages will undoubtedly impress an employer as someone who is capable of organizing a much larger work project.

WHAT GOES INTO A RESUME

A resume must contain a certain amount of essential information. Although this information varies from person to person, several categories are standard in any resume:

1. A heading, which may be as simple as the word "Resume" at the top of the page or as complicated as a well-thought-out "Job Objective" that describes the type of position you hope to obtain
2. Your name, address, city, state, and phone numbers where you can be reached
3. A job title or objective if that was not part of the title and if that applies to the type of work you seek
4. A detailed record of your employment history
5. A detailed record of your education
6. Any languages you know
7. Anything you have published, either magazine or journal articles or books, if this is pertinent to the work you do
8. Any relevant professional memberships
9. A record of your military service
10. Any personal information you feel is important and choose to include
11. A statement to the effect that your references and any samples of your work, if that applies to the kind of work you do, are available on request

This is the maximum number of items that would appear on a resume. Few persons will choose to use all these categories. Knowing which categories you should choose is part of the knack of resume writing.

Let's take a look at each of these items in greater detail.

The Heading.   In many instances, as already noted, the heading of your resume can simply be the word "Resume." Or you might write "Resume of [fill in your name]." Some persons choose to use their name as the heading for the resume; others use a job title or objective. The point is that there should be some identifying line at the top of the resume—some clue to the reader that lets him know what he is about to read.

If most of your resumes will be going to contacts, your name may be the best heading. If most of your resumes will be going to unknown personnel directors, a job title may be the best approach.

Name, Address, Phone Numbers.   Your name, address, city, state, and phone numbers may seem too irrelevant to mention, but this information is vital—and too often forgotten. The personnel director of a Fortune 500 company reported his frustration at receiving the perfect resume from what appeared to be the perfectly qualified candidate for a very high-level management position—only to discover that it contained no name or address. Failing to include your name and address is a fatal mistake—no one can call you or write you to tell you that you omitted it. Also, it is important to include your zip code and telephone area code if you will be applying for jobs out of your state or community.

Deciding what telephone number to put on your resume can pose a problem. Obviously, you will not be in a position to take many calls about job possibilities while you are at work. In fact, some employers have admitted to being hesitant about hiring someone who can talk for hours during the work day. Possibly the best solution is to list your present office number and your home number. When you are called during the day, keep the call as brief as possible and ask if you can call back during the evening or your lunch hour. No one expects you to jeopardize your present job for a future one, so most prospective employers will be understanding and cooperative about making arrangements for you to call back. Also, the presence of your home phone indicates that you can be reached after work hours. Most of the callers responding to your resume will be prepared to save most of the talking for the interview and will expect only a brief telephone conversation to set up the interview, particularly if they have called you at work.

Job Title or Objective.   Most resumes need either a job title or a job objective. A job title, if you choose to use one, should be a simple one- or two-word description of what you do—speech therapist, technical writer, paramedic. A job title usually reflects your present level of skills rather than what you hope to do next. The one exception is the job title for a new college graduate, who should, of course, note what he or she hopes to do. Putting "College Graduate" down as a job title would be silly.

If you are hoping to make a sizable jump in responsibilities, a job objective may be more appropriate for your resume. A job objective also works well for a college graduate seeking an entry-level position. It should be used, in short, when you feel you would like to do a little more explaining about your needs. A job objective can be less defining than a job title, or it can be very specific about stating what you hope to obtain in your next position. If, for example, you are job hunting in a favorable job market, you may want a fairly open, vague job objective that will cause employers to consider you for a variety of jobs. Still, not every resume must have a job objective. If you find that your job objective is too vague to be useful, do not include it.

In a tight job market, you might do better to write a more specific job objective—one that is geared exactly to the job you know you want. Specialists and highly trained technicians generally do better with a fairly specific job objective; if you fall into this category, the range of work you do is fairly well defined, and there is little point in leaving yourself open to positions that you have no intention of filling.

A job objective should be clearly labeled as such. It should be concise and definitive, and probably should not run more than three to five lines.

Here is a sample job objective for a laboratory technician:

> **Job Objective:** A position as a senior technician with a middle-sized chemical or drug firm where I can continue my research in cancer.

A teacher's job objective might look like this:

> **Job Objective:** To work with grade-school children in a creative social sciences program in an experimental school.

A nurse's resume might carry this job objective:

> **Job Objective:** Employment in an outpatient clinic that emphasizes family and group counseling.

A new business school graduate might cite the following objective:

> **Job Objective:** A managerial training position with a bank.

Employment Record.   After the job title comes your employment record. There are several ways to write this, depending upon the type of resume format you choose. You could begin with your most recent job and work back to the first, or first relevant, position. Or you could describe the work you have done or your accomplishments in one section and give a brief chronology in another section. This is a technique favored by over-forty managerial persons and

4

persons who are looking for a first job—in each case, age might be held against the person, and the achievements are stressed before the chronology is presented.

Your resume must include the dates of your employment. If it does not, many personnel workers will toss it out. Also, if possible, give the exact dates of each employment; include the days if you can, but definitely give the month and year, or the years alone if you have worked for many years. If one item is consistently checked on a resume, it is the dates of employment, and it is not worth the risk to misrepresent them.

If there are gaps in your employment record due to illness or unemployment, there is no reason to try to cover them up. Simply omit these years on the resume and explain them honestly if they are brought up during an interview.

You need not give a description of every job you have ever held, particularly if you have worked for a long time. As you gain more experience, list only the jobs that are relevant. A prospective employer reads a resume to see what you have been doing, not where you have been doing it.

Education. After your employment record comes your educational background. If you are a professional, begin with your most recent education. If you stopped attending school after high school, list your high school first.

A good guideline in describing your education is to give the most details about the schooling that most directly applies to the position you hope to obtain. A person holding a doctorate in American history needs to mention only the name of his high school and the year of graduation. Far more important are his academic credentials beyond high school. A graduate of a vocational school should give the greater share of space to describing his vocational training and should not include many details of his high school education.

Generally, begin with your most recent educational experience and work your way backward in time.

Grade standing, unless important to your career field, need not be mentioned. But law-school graduates, for example, are expected to mention class standing on a resume. A literature major need not. You certainly should not mention class standing if it will not work in your favor.

School honors and organizations, too, need not be mentioned unless they are important to your career.

A recent graduate would be more inclined to mention academic honors or extracurricular activities, because they are all he has to sell. As work experience is gained, such items should be dropped from the resume.

If you have taken or are taking night-school courses to update your skills, they are important to mention on a resume, as are seminars, workshops, conferences, and other career-related educational activities you may be involved in.

5

Languages. After education, note any languages that you know and the level of proficiency.

Publications. In some fields, notably academia, published works are important and should be noted on a resume. Go for quality rather than quantity, however, if you have published a great deal. Too many academic resumes run on for pages listing publications— so many, in fact, that it soon becomes apparent that lots of graduate students had to be helping out. Far better simply to state that you have published x number of articles and to list a few of the more impressive journals in which you are published than to detail 200 articles published over the past ten years.

Academic credits should include the title of the work, publishers, date of publication, and city of publication. Journal or magazine articles include a volume number and issue date, if noted on the publication. A good stylebook (see bibliography) contains details on writing a publishing credit note.

Professional Memberships. Mention only those memberships that are directly relevant to your work skills. Community or church participation are no longer considered pertinent items to include on a resume. Do not go into great detail about these activities, or you may give the impression that your after-work activities could cut into your work hours.

Military Service. List the branch of service, dates of service, rank at time of discharge, and briefly state what you did in the service.

Personal Information. Personal information is a little tricky these days. Legally, prospective employers can ask you very little about yourself, and you do not have to supply any personal information such as marital status, plans regarding children, or age. One subtle way to exchange this information, however, is to put it on a resume. On the other hand, if your age might work against you, why announce it in advance? Obviously, once you are on an interview, the interviewer can readily judge your age. But if you write an otherwise sound resume with no mention of your age, you may have a better chance of getting the interview.

A good rule of thumb is to include the bare minimum of personal information that will be required for you to obtain an interview.

If you are comfortable including personal information, the most you will probably want to include is your birth date (not your age, which changes every year), marital status, willingness to relocate, and willingness to travel. Obviously, no mention should be made of the fact that you are not willing to relocate or travel.

Too many persons include too much information about their families. The names and ages of your children will not help you get a job, for example, nor will a listing of your wife's accomplishments.

Other personal information you include in your resume should have a direct bearing on the work you hope to do. If you are applying for work with an international firm and you have lived in Spain and are fluent in two languages besides English, for example, this is personal information that definitely should be included.

References and Portfolio.   The final section of your resume is a mere formality—a statement that you will and can supply references if and when the job looks definite enough for a prospective employer to start checking out these things. Persons who work in creative fields should also be prepared to present samples of their work, often referred to as a portfolio.

Arranging the Information

The order of these categories of information will vary from resume to resume. Usually it appears in the order in which it was just described. If your academic credentials are very important, though, you might continue to present them ahead of work history for several years.

Personal information might appear right after your name and address or at the very end of the resume. These are questions of choice that relate more to the look of the resume and the actual information than to any arbitrary way of doing things.

Generally, when listing work experience and education, begin with your most recent experience.

Because it is so important not to omit any pertinent information, a checklist of the categories of information is included in chapter 5. Use it for the final check when you have finished writing your resume and before you have it professionally typed.

2 MAKING YOUR RESUME LOOK GOOD

Editors and typographers have long been aware that some combinations of words on a printed page look more attractive than others do. While it is impossible to develop the keen eye of a typographer without training, you can acquire a few guidelines for organizing the way a resume looks to ensure that it will be pleasing to the eye of the reader.

RESUME STYLES

There are several accepted kinds of resumes. The most common kind—and the one most useful to personnel persons—is the historical-chronological resume. In this type of resume, you present your work and educational histories in chronological order, beginning with your most recent experience.

Even if you have decided to use one of the other two forms for your resume, it is probably a good idea to prepare a chronological resume, simply because it forms a good basis for any spin-off resumes you may want to write.

Remember, too, that the chronological resume merely puts the dates in your life up front; all other resumes must also contain the times when you worked in various places and when you attended school. Resumes without this vital information are often discarded without even one serious reading. On page 10 is an example of a historical-chronological resume.

The second widely accepted type of resume is the skills- or achievement-oriented resume. It emphasizes skills and achievement

PARKER M. SMITHFIELD III
855 Baker Street
Evanston, Illinois 60202
Telephone: (Residence) 312-480-8594 (Office) 312-560-8000

PERSONAL

Will relocate
Willing to travel

EMPLOYMENT HISTORY

1/73 to
present

ABC Publishing Company, sponsoring editor, modern languages
and education. I have contracted for thirty books: twenty-
five in modern languages and five in education. I have
transformed the education list from a collection of small-
market supplementary texts into a well-developed, competitive
list of basic, undergraduate texts.

1/65 to
1/73

American Textbook Development Company, managing editor
As managing editor, I planned and conducted one- and two-day
workshops to present and demonstrate new modern language
publications and programs to high school teachers and
administrators and to college instructors. Sales in the
northeast territory increased 40 percent during my tenure.

I also directed, developed, and administered the publishing
program and staff selection, training, and supervision.

EDUCATIONAL BACKGROUND

1966-1968   Temple University Graduate School, attended at night,
M.A., anthropology

1961-1965   Temple University, B.A., French

1960-1961   American College in Paris, liberal arts

I have also attended employer-sponsored graduate seminars in programmed
instruction, applied linguistics, and language teaching methods.

above chronological events. This type of resume is used mostly by professionals in business, banking, and academic and scientific fields. It is useful any time you wish to sell a specialized or technical skill that is more important than the chronological events of your work history. On page 12 is an example of a skills-oriented resume.

The third kind of resume—a creative one—is trickier to do, mostly because it is so easily overdone. Creative resumes are useful for artists, typesetters, and others in the graphic arts, advertising, or merchandising. They sometimes work well for a person who is changing fields or a woman returning to work after staying home for several years.

A creative resume must be truly clever rather than cute. It must relate to one specific point about yourself—showing off your skills as an artist, for example, or stressing that you are hoping to change fields. It should not attempt to be clever throughout—television sitcoms rarely manage to be clever for an entire show, and there is even less chance that you can do it in a resume. Make your clever point, grab attention, and then back off and present yourself in a fairly staid way in the rest of the resume.

Creative resumes are not acceptable in fields such as business, banking, science, law, and academia. An example of a creative resume appears on page 14.

Other Kinds of Resumes

Two other kinds of resumes may prove useful on occasion. The first is the capsule resume, and the second is the letter resume.

A capsule resume is a one-page summary of your work experience and possibly your education. It is intended to grab the reader, not to present all the facts about you. A capsule resume should always be backed up by a chronological-historical resume.

Sometimes a person may send a capsule resume with a cover letter indicating that a more detailed resume is available; more often a capsule resume and a chronological-historical resume are used together. An example of a capsule resume appears on page 15.

A letter resume, which is merely resume information summarized in letter form, usually is sent to someone who knows you fairly well. In the letter, which should be typed and should follow the standard format of a business letter, state your familiarity with the company's needs and how you might successfully fill a certain position. You may want to enclose a more detailed resume.

A letter resume works when a company does not have an opening but might create one to meet your skills. On page 16 is an example of a letter resume.

PARKER M. SMITHFIELD III
855 Baker Street
Evanston, Illinois 60202
Telephone: (Residence) 312-448-8594 (Office) 312-560-8000

OBJECTIVE

A senior editorial product development position in the social/behavioral sciences in college textbook publishing. I am qualified to acquire and develop major-market undergraduate textbooks in psychology, sociology, anthropology, education, and modern languages.

SUMMARY

I am currently sponsoring/acquiring editor at ABC Publishing Company and am responsible for texts in education and modern languages. I am also involved in marketing, advertising, and promotion activities. Prior to joining ABC Publishing Company, I worked for eight years for American Textbook Development Company as managing editor. I gained experience in sales and marketing, editorial, and management.

ACHIEVEMENTS

Sales. I developed, planned, and conducted one- and two-day workshops to present and demonstrate new modern-language publications and programs to high school teachers and administrators and to college instructors. Sales in the northeast territory increased 40 percent during my tenure. As a consequence of the success of the workshops, the company adopted this approach as the primary marketing strategy.

Managerial. As managing editor of the American Textbook Development Company, I directed, developed, and administered the publishing program and staff selection, training, and supervision.

Editorial. While working at ABC Publishing Company, I have contracted for thirty books: twenty-five in modern languages and five in education. I have transformed the education list from a collection of small-market, supplementary texts into a well-developed, competitive list of basic undergraduate texts.

Product Development. I have established new approaches, systems, and procedures in product development at ABC Publishing Company, and have developed a step-by-step approach to planning, conceptualizing, and evaluating new textbook projects.

EMPLOYMENT HISTORY

From 1-73
to present

ABC Publishing Company, sponsoring editor, modern languages and education.

From 1-65
to 1-73

American Textbook Development Company, managing editor.

EDUCATIONAL BACKGROUND

1966-1968

Temple University, graduate school, attended at night, M.A., anthropology

1961-1965

Temple University, B.A., French

1960-1961

American College in Paris, liberal arts

I have also attended employer-sponsored graduate seminars in programmed instruction, applied linguistics, and language teaching methods.

ATTENTION,

COLLEGE TEXTBOOK PUBLISHERS!

Are you looking for creativity, managerial skills, and a proven track record? I may be the man you are looking for.

I CAN OFFER THE FOLLOWING:

. Sales in the northeast territory increased 40 percent during my tenure at one publishing company.

. I developed, planned, and conducted one- and two-day workshops to present and demonstrate new modern-language publications and programs to high school teachers and administrators and to college instructors. The company has adopted this approach as its primary marketing strategy.

. I have directed, developed, and administered the publishing program and staff selection, training, and supervision of a major college textbook publishing house.

. I have contracted for thirty books: twenty-five in modern languages and five in education, turning one publisher's list from a collection of small-market, supplementary texts into a well-developed, competitive list of basic undergraduate texts.

. I have developed a step-by-step approach to planning, conceptualizing, and evaluating new textbook projects.

IF YOU, TOO, THINK I MIGHT BE THE MAN YOU
ARE LOOKING FOR, LET'S TALK.

PARKER M. SMITHFIELD III
855 Baker Street
Evanston, Illinois 60202
Telephone: (Residence) 312-448-8594   (Office) 312-560-8000

14

Parker M. Smithfield III
855 Baker Street
Evanston, Illinois 60202
Telephone: (Residence) 312-448-8594 (Office) 312-560-8000

OBJECTIVES

A senior editorial/product development position in the social/behavioral
sciences in college textbook publishing. I am qualified to acquire and
develop major market, undergraduate textbooks in psychology, sociology,
anthropology, education, and modern languages. I am especially interested
in applications of survey/market research in conceptualizing and developing a new product and have been involved in recent efforts in my present
position to investigate new product development systems and procedures.

SUMMARY

I am currently a sponsoring/acquiring editor at ABC Publishing Company and
am responsible for texts in education and modern languages. I am also
involved in marketing, advertising, and promotional activities for education and modern language texts. Prior to joining this firm, I was the
managing editor of the American Textbook Development Company, where I had
eight years in sales and marketing, editorial, and management.

Parker M. Smithfield III
855 Baker Street
Evanston, Illinois 60202
April 3, 19—

Ms. Adele Skinner
4500 Skokie Boulevard
Modern Textbooks, Inc., Publishers
Cleveland, Ohio 44122

Dear Adele:

It was pleasant talking with you last week at the Modern Language
Convention, and I would be interested in talking with you further about
the possibility of a position in editorial at Modern Textbooks, Inc.

As you know, my present position is in editorial and product development. While I am currently acquiring in education and modern languages,
I am qualified to acquire in psychology, sociology, and anthropology.

Prior to going to work for my present company, I spent eight years
with the American Textbook Development Company, where I worked in sales
and marketing, editorial and management.

One of my major interests--and one in which I am gaining a lot of
experience these days--is in the application of survey-market research
to conceptualizing and developing new products.

Well, Adele, this is pretty much the rough sketch of my past work
history. I hope it interests you and that we can meet quite soon to
talk more about the opening.

Again, it was great seeing you. I wish you luck in your new
position--the company is lucky to have you on its team.

Cordially,

Parker M. Smithfield III

16

The format of a resume refers to how it looks physically. A great deal of thought must be given to the physical arrangement of a resume. It should be easy to read, compact, and probably not more than three pages. If you are having difficulty fitting what you have to say into this number of pages, you may be trying to say too much. Go over the information one more time to see if there is anything else you can take out.

Leave a sizable margin—one to one and a half inches—all around, and leave a fair amount of space between categories of information.

A resume should be written on white or pale-colored bond paper or other paper of good quality. Pale colors are less conservative than white, but they are acceptable in most places. Buff, light brown, manila, and pale gray are colors you may choose from. Probably the best reason for using colored paper is that it coordinates with your stationery. But in most conservative fields, such as banking, business, and law, white paper is still safest.

A resume should be printed on paper 8½ by 11 inches. It should be at least twenty-pound weight so as not to appear skimpy. Go to heavier paper—up to sixty-pound—if your resume is one-page long. A resume that runs two or three pages should be on lighter-weight paper or mailing it will become a problem; you will find yourself spending money for extra postage and buying large envelopes. Sometimes resumes are printed on copy-machine paper; this is fine if the paper is high enough in quality.

Single space the resume and double- or triple-space between categories of information. Because a single-spaced copy is sometimes hard to read, try to organize all the type in your resume carefully to ensure that it is easy to read and attractive to the eye. Study the examples that follow. Which ones look least cluttered to you? Which resume has the most pleasing appearance?

Resume 1 is the most pleasing to the eye, because it follows standard guidelines used by graphic designers and typesetters to organize type for magazines, books, and other printed materials. The white margins are equal on the top and two sides and slightly larger at the bottom. Identical heads are used to introduce parallel sections of information. It also makes the most efficient use of space.

Resume 2 is cluttered looking. The margins are too small; the arrangement of type on the page appears to follow no set pattern. Initially, subheads are aligned with the left margin; then they are in the center of the page. All in all, this is a messy-looking resume, better avoided.

Resume 3 won't hurt the reader's eyes, but it does waste valuable space that might better be put to use selling your job skills. This is a popular format and actually works fairly well for a one-page resume. If your resume tends to run long or if you have a lot to say, you may want to avoid this format.

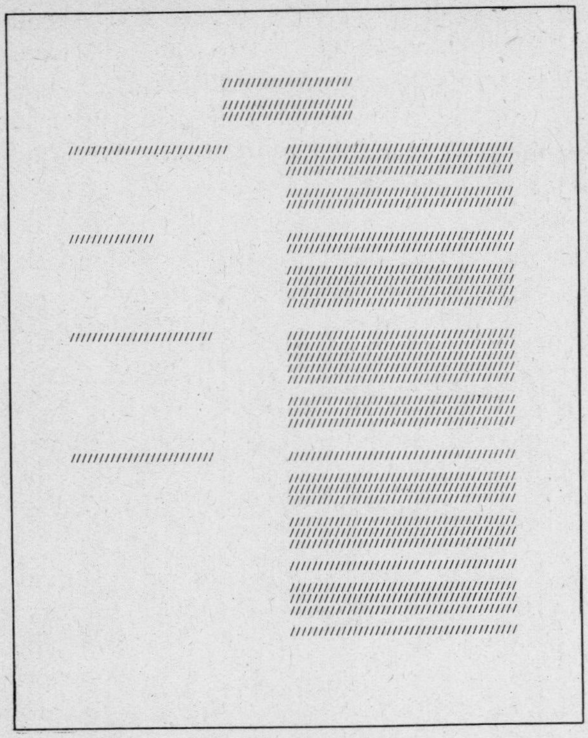

1

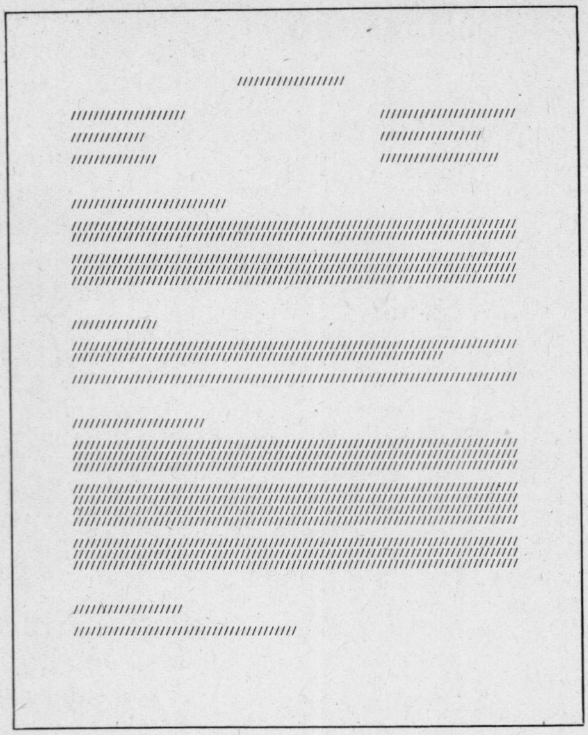

2

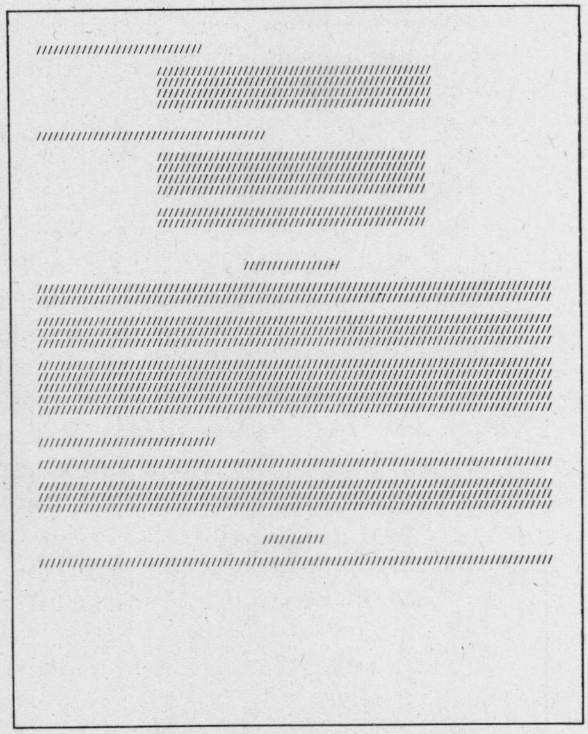

3

Try to draw a rough sketch of your resume once you have culled enough information so that you can begin to visualize how you might arrange it. The resume may turn out different when you actually type it, but drawing such a sketch will give you an idea where copy blocks should go and how much space to allot for everything.

Using Headlines to Divide the Resume

To plan the format of your resume, decide what headlines or identification lines you will need. The most obvious head you will need is the word "Resume" or your name in bold type. Sometimes "Vita" or "Curriculum Vitae" is used instead of "Resume,' but this is done mostly by academics. This is the major head, and it should stand out more than any other head on the page. You will probably want to put it in capital letters or in capital letters and small letters with underlining.

Draw up a list of other heads you will need—usually these include Education, Work History or Employment, Personal, Honors or Professional Honors, Publications, and Military Service. These heads are all similar—that is, they introduce blocks of descriptive copy—so they should all be identical. You can choose to underline them, capitalize them, put them flush left or right or center them on the page; just make sure that they are all exactly alike and in the same position.

Organizing Information Blocks

The next step is to organize the information blocks that will go under the heads. Anything not used to label a section is an information block; the information blocks are the paragraphs that contain information about your education, work history, and so on.

They should be organized to look as much alike as possible. There will be some problems: for example, the sections on your employment history and your education will contain dates, whereas the personal-information section and the professional-honors section may not. Just remember that the dates must be done in exactly the same way in all sections with dates.

Information blocks may be written in paragraph form as follows:

October 1955-June 1961, ABC Company

After a six-month training period, I went to work in the department responsible for purchasing machine parts. I was promoted to assistant buyer for machine parts in 1958. In 1959, I assumed direction of all buying for company.

Information blocks may be organized into lists, as follows:

1963-1967   Duke University, B.A., literature
1967-1969   Indiana University, M.A., cultural anthropology

19

These two examples show several points you need to consider when planning your resume. First, decide whether you want information blocks indented and if so, how much they will be indented. You can also decide what kind of indents you want. You can indent the first line three to five spaces, as follows:

> Established new approaches, systems, and procedures in
> product development at ABC Publishing Company. Developed
> a step-by-step approach to planning . . .

You can use a hanging indent, in which the first line is flush left and the remaining lines are indented, as follows:

> Established new approaches, systems, and procedures in product
> development at ABC Publishing Company. Developed a
> step-by-step approach to planning . . .

Or you can decide not to indent at all and to use extra space to separate the paragraphs. Whatever you do, be consistent—do exactly the same thing to every paragraph.

Second, decide whether you want to use periods at the end of information blocks. Since complete sentences usually end with periods, the answer is nearly always yes. But if you have several lists that are not complete sentences, you should omit periods. Here is an example of a list where periods would be silly:

> <u>Skills</u>
>
> > IBM Selectric typewriter—80 w.p.m.
> > Pitman shorthand
> > Dictaphone
> > Adding machine
> > Office calculator

Try to keep information blocks similar in size. If one does run longer than the others, it should be the one describing your most recent position. Detailed descriptions of early jobs should gradually be pared down as you gain more experience.

Once you have decided what goes into each information block, how you will indent it, and whether you will use periods at the end, decide whether you want to emphasize anything within the block. In your employment section, for example, you will probably want to emphasize the title of the jobs you have held, as follows:

> December 1958-November 1963   Senior editor

Or you might write:

> Senior editor, Olympia Publishing, 1958-1963

The best way to add emphasis within an information block is to underline; capital letters are too strong.

Be careful about adding too much emphasis, though. Most people make that mistake in a resume. Underline only those words or numbers that you truly want to stand out—those items that are very important to you and to a prospective employer.

The best way to learn about resume formats is to study other resumes and magazines and books to see how the type is handled in them. Gradually you will develop an eye for what looks pleasing on the printed page and what looks messy.

3

MODEL RESUMES

Resumes are highly personal, and you will not be able to copy a resume from this book for your own use. By reading all the resumes carefully, however, you may obtain hints on how to write a resume or even a particular paragraph that has been troubling you.

Each resume is titled with the kind of job that is described in that resume. At the end of almost every resume is a brief list of other jobs for which that resume could be used.

MASTER RESUME INDEX

25

27

ACCOUNTANT-AUDITOR

RESUME OF MARY DALEY   CERTIFIED PUBLIC ACCOUNTANT

1288 Shortridge Drive
Raleigh, North Carolina 27605
222-1597

Will travel   Will relocate

JOB OBJECTIVE

Position as comptroller for small- to middle-sized services-oriented firm.

WORK EXPERIENCE

Treasurer, GHI Products, Inc., Columbus, North Carolina. 1972 to present.
In addition to my usual responsibilities as treasurer, I have reorganized
the billing system, which has resulted in an annual savings of $35,000 to
the firm.

Manager of internal auditing, HHH Insurance Co., Hillside, South Carolina.
1968 to 1972. Responsible for seven corporate accounts. Supervised staff
of eighteen. Instituted new office procedures to eliminate paperwork and
save time for staff.

Internal auditor, senior level, HHH Insurance Co. 1967 to 1968.

Internal auditor, trainee, HHH Insurance Co. 1965 to 1967.

EDUCATION and HONORS

B.A., accounting, Johnsville State University, Johnsville, South Carolina,
1967.

Became Certified Public Accountant, 1973.

Member of Financial Women's Executives Association; served as vice president in charge of membership.

REFERENCES

Available on request.

*Bank executive, financial manager,
internal auditor, public
accountant, tax accountant*

ADVERTISING ACCOUNT EXECUTIVE

Daniel Fitzsimons

LOOKING FOR BUSINESS ACUMEN, TALENT, AND MORE PROFITS?

I may be the person you seek. For example:

BUSINESS ACUMEN

M.A., Florida State University, advertising marketing, 1970.

B.A., Tennessee State, major in advertising and minor in business administration, 1968.

TALENT AND PROFITS

Worked five years for major advertising firm as junior and then senior account executive. Created complete advertising campaign for five major corporate clients, three of whom I wooed away from other agencies.

Worked six years as senior account executive for major advertising agency. I brought three of five major accounts with me and organized completely new, successful campaigns for them. In addition, I brought in three new corporate accounts, for a total of $500,700 annual extra earnings for the firm.

WORK CHRONOLOGY

Fedder Advertising Company, November 1970 to August 1979.

A-1 Advertising Agency, June 1968 to August 1970.

REFERENCES AND SAMPLES

Available on request.

IF YOU THINK WE NEED EACH OTHER, PLEASE CONTACT ME AT:

800 North Avenue
Chicago, Illinois 60611
Telephone: 312-847-8376

Executive, market researcher,
creative resume.

ADVERTISING ASSISTANT — New Graduate

MARGIE RUBENSTEIN

123 Evans Avenue
Iowa City, Iowa 52242
(319) 348-6666

Available after May 16, 1979
1001 Eighteenth Avenue
(515) 858-3174

JOB OBJECTIVE:
Advertising-assistant position with possible advancement to a career as an account executive.

EDUCATION:
B.A., May 1979, University of Iowa. Concentrations in Journalism and Marketing. Earned 50% of college expenses.

Course Highlights: Marketing Communications, Consumer Behavior, Theory/ Practice of Persuasion, Advertising Theory/Planning, News Editing, Graphic Arts, Organizing Mass Communication Productions.

EXPERIENCE:
Advertising and Reporting: Advertising Intern (Summer 1978), Sun Newspapers of Omaha. Responsibilities were handling and servicing various account departments, the advertising director's accounts, designing and laying out ads, selling ad space, and working in traffic control. Feature Reporter (Summer 1977), Eldora Herald Index. Wrote feature articles, covered city council meetings, set headlines, sold and laid out advertising for a special insert. Stencil Designer (Summer 1975, 1976), Dodger Gym Manufacturing. Designed in-house stencils for customer orders and stenciled athletic wear. Standing job with Dodger Gym for all semester and spring breaks.

Other Work Experience: Hostess/Waitress, Shipping Department, Crew Boss.

PUBLICATIONS/PROJECTS:
Feature stories, Eldora Herald Index; two articles, School of Journalism Lab Tabs; editor of a four-page tabloid; editor of a marketing-research analysis project for Hardee's; advertisements, Eldora Herald Index and the Sun Newspapers; now in progress, twenty-minute documentary in film.

HONORS/AWARDS:
University of Iowa athletic scholarship, scholarship loan from Miriam Brown Educational Trust Fund, Dolphin Queen candidate.

Advertising Copywriter, media trainee

(Continued)

COLLEGE ACTIVITIES:
Member/team captain of Women's Intercollegiate Basketball Team, intra-
mural athletics, selected member of Greek Expansion Task Force, publica-
tions/historian Pi Beta Phi, March of Dimes Fund Drive.

PERSONAL:
Single; 22; no geographical preference.

Strengths: energetic, work well under pressure, very willing to accept
responsibility, have great perseverance.

REFERENCES/PORTFOLIO:
References available at Career Services and Placement Center, Iowa
Memorial Union, University of Iowa, Iowa City, Iowa 52242,
(319) 353-3147. Portfolio available upon request.

AIRLINE RESERVATIONIST

R E S U M E

O F

A L I C E   O D E L L

I have two years experience as a reservationist on a major domestic airline, a pleasant appearance, a personality that works well with the public,
and a good speaking voice.

I am seeking a position with an international airlines as a ticket agent.
Additional details about my skills and education are listed below. If
you believe I am the person you are looking for, won't you test my speaking voice by calling

405-738-9386

WORK EXPERIENCE

August 1976-present. Employed with United Airlines as a phone reservationist for twelve months. For past twelve months, I have worked as a
ticket agent in a major downtown travel center, where I handle off-the-
street traffic as well as phone inquiries about travel plans.

CAREER TRAINING

One-week training course at professional airlines school in Tallahassee,
Florida.

Four weeks on-the-job training by United Airlines.

One-week seminar on "Using Computers in Reservations Work."

EDUCATION

Associate degree, Truman Junior College, Chicago, Illinois, June 1976.

Graduated Eden High School, Chicago, Illinois, June 1974.

PERSONAL INTERESTS

Travel, championship swimmer in high school and college, reading, sewing.

43 East Eighty-third Street, New York, New York   10022

*Airline flight attendant,
reservations clerk, travel agent*

33

ARCHITECT

KARL VOORHEES
3250 LAKE SHORE DRIVE, APT. 2203
CHICAGO, ILLINOIS 60657
PHONE: 312-587-9481

Job Objective

Position with firm nationally recognized for its work in urban renewal and preservation.

Employment History

<u>1974 to present</u>: Alpha Architectural Associates, Chicago, Illinois. Junior partner. Responsibilities include developing initial plans and recommendations to be presented to firm's board of directors; drawing up final plans for clients once preliminary plans have been approved by board; and presenting plans, under supervision of senior partner, to clients and municipal boards responsible for approving building plans. Depending upon the project, I am responsible for anywhere from five to thirty persons. For two years, I assumed responsibility for three to five student interns working in office.

<u>1969-1974</u>: Graham Architects and Urban Planners. Specification writer. Responsibilities included preparing directions and explanations of architect's plans to be used by builders and others working on construction, proposal writing for new projects, and heavy involvement in the planning and construction stages of the Jacksonville County Courthouse renovation.

<u>1965-1969</u>: Murphy and Lyons, Associates. Junior drafter. Rendered models and architectural drawings for use by firm.

Education

<u>1960-1965</u>: University of Michigan, master of architecture, five-year program. Two summers, as part of the program, were spent as an intern in C. Fondette and Des Pres, Inc., both in Chicago. Spent junior year studying architectural history in Florence, Italy.

<u>1960</u>: Arlington City High School, Arlington, Virginia. Graduated with honors.

Electrical engineer, executive, mechanical artist, mechanical engineer, urban planner

34

Professional Data

Licensed by State of Illinois, 1969.
Consultant to Landmarks, Inc., a publicly funded organization devoted to preserving public buildings of architectural and historic value.

Personal

Married, two children
Will relocate.
Interests include collecting old architecture books and public restoration projects.

Military

U.S. Navy, 1958-1960. Discharged with rank of lieutenant. Worked in intelligence. Attended OCS.

ART DIRECTOR

WALTER JUSTIN

1190 Gulf Lane   Phone: 312-756-7309
Park Ridge, Illinois 60068   312-744-7590

JOB OBJECTIVE

Position as senior art director in large urban advertising agency.

CAPSULE

My primary activity as art director has been to supervise the creative
work on various advertising projects. I have carried as many as ten
accounts at one time and have worked on five major cigarette accounts
(at various times), one car account, and two major cosmetic accounts.
Responsibilities include: hiring and working with layout artists, copywriters, and designers, and supervising an in-house creative team. In
all the accounts I have handled, I have been a primary force in generat-
ing and developing advertising ideas, and I consider the ability to do
this one of my major strengths.

CHRONOLOGICAL RECORD

J. Christopher Agency, 1975-present. Hired as assistant art director
when this agency was less than one year old, I have progressed to art
director and the agency has tripled in size and become an important
force in the advertising world.

EDUCATION

Art Institute of Chicago, B.A., fine arts, 1973.
Lived in Paris, France, studied at Sorbonne, 1974.

PORTFOLIO AND REFERENCES

Available on request.

*Advertising assistant, advertising
executive, advertising media buyer,
advertising production manager,
freelance artist, media manager*

ATTORNEY

Amelia Baker
80 River Road
Princeton, New Jersey 08540

Personal

Telephone: 857-9476
Single
Will travel
Will relocate

Job Objective

Position as senior counsel with federal government agency, preferably one with special interest in affirmative action.

Experience

5/70 to present: Counsel, Mayor's Council on Affirmative Action Responsible for reviewing corporate employment records to ensure equal opportunity for employees. Sued five major corporations, winning back pay for employees in three of the cases. Reviewed contracts between city government agencies and private corporations to ensure that federal standards for fair employment were being met. Supervised staff of five.

Education

Columbia University, 1963, B.A., international politics.
New York University, 1969, LL.B.
Class standing: 20 out of 230.

Interests

Since 1970, have volunteered two evenings a week as counselor for Woman's Agency, a privately funded foundation that counsels women who have been discriminated against at work.

References

Furnished on request.

Legal-aid worker, lobbyist

BANK TELLER

MARGARET EBERT
8380 Green Avenue, S.W.
Washington, D.C. 20023
Phone: 202-837-8291

Job Title

Bank Teller

Work Experience

Commercial Teller

First Federal Savings & Loan
Washington, D.C.
October 1973-Present
Three weeks special training in
use of computer terminal.

Assistant Note Teller

National Boulevard Bank
Washington, D.C.
April 1972-October 1973

Education

Saugatauk Junior College, one year, business administration
Saugatauk High School, graduated January 1972. Took business curriculum.

Interests

People, music, reading, travel

Accounting trainee, accounts-receivable clerk, billing clerk, note teller

BOOKKEEPER

<u>Accounting Clerk</u>

Victoria Taylor
600 Mill Road
Hyattsville, Maryland 20782
Phone: 958-9584

<u>Employment Record</u>

Statements Clerk
H.M. Sanders, Accountants, 1976 to present

Major responsibility: preparing periodic statements reports for four major clients. Also assist with internal auditing for these firms.

Bookkeeper
Henderson, Inc., 1975-1976

Responsible for wide variety of functions: maintaining ledger records, accounts receivable on daily sales, payroll deductions, some routine clerical work such as typing vouchers, invoices, and other records. Was hired as a secretary to operations vice president, promoted to bookkeeper after four months.

<u>Education</u>

Delaware Junior College, associate degree in business and bookkeeping, 1975
Delaware Central High School, business course, graduated 1973.

<u>Skills</u>

Familiar with most accounting-related business machines
Typing
Shorthand

<u>Personal</u>

Married, divorced, no children
Will relocate, will travel

Accounting trainee, accounts-receivable clerk, billing clerk, file clerk, hospital billing clerk

CARPENTER

Tom MacFarlane
1930 Clinton Avenue East
San Jose, New Mexico 87565
Phone: 328-0070

Summary

Seek employment as carpenter; have extensive training and am capable of either rough or finished work. Specialize in building new houses.

Job Training

Apprentice in Carpenters' Program, sponsored by local union. Involved four years of on-the-job training plus 144 hours of classroom instruction. 1952-1956.

Hightower Architectural Company. Worked two years in drafting and blueprint reading. 1950-1951.

Mountain Black High School. Vocational course in carpentry. Each year the senior class built a house as its project. I served as carpentry foreman. 1946-1950.

Job Experience

Worked various construction sites, 1956 to present. For past six years, have worked as carpenters' foreman for Grimstead Construction, San Ildefonso, New Mexico.

References

Furnished on request.

Building-trades worker, electrician, construction foreman, supervisor, tool and die maker

CASHIER

RESUME

Suzanne Goodman
Phone: 938-8371

893 Eaton Place
Onawa, Maine 04470

JOB OBJECTIVE: Cashier in grocery store or other retail store

WORK HISTORY: Cash and Carry Department Store
                 Chicago, Illinois
                 April 1973 to present

                 Sloan's Vegetable Mart
                 Chicago, Illinois
                 August 1972-April 1973

                 Pay Less Groceries
                 Chicago, Illinois
                 Part-time while attending high school
                 September 1968-June 1972

SKILLS: Familiar with optical and magnetic scanner
                 Familiar with all office functions of grocery
                   store, such as exchange forms, change forms,
                   receipts
                 Familiar with adding machine
                 Familiar with point-of-change terminals

EDUCATION: Knob Hill High School
                 Graduated June 1972
                 Studied business and office-skills course

REFERENCES: Available on request

Bank teller, retail salesperson

41

CHEF

RESUME

Mark Jones
800 Mountain Drive   Phones: 487-1100 (home)
San Francisco, California 94102   555-4444 (office)

_____

Job Objective: Position as dessert chef in kitchen of restaurant recognized for standards of excellence in food preparation.

_____

Employment: Sauce and dessert chef, alternate shifts, Mountainside View Resort, since 1976.

Chief lunch chef, ABC Quik Foods, Inc., Oregon City, 1974-1976.

Junior dessert chef, Whitesides Hotel, Chicago, 1971-1974.

_____

Education: Oregon City Vocational High School program for
professional cooking and restaurant management, graduated
January 1971.

_____

Personal: Will travel; will relocate; would be particularly
interested in metropolitan area.

*Counter/short-order cook, food
services worker, restaurant
manager*

COMMERCIAL ARTIST

David Eaves
444 Riverside Lane
Kansas City, Kansas 66106
Telephone: 837-8371

SUMMARY

Commercial artist specializing in finished illustration, known for cartoon style.

WORK EXPERIENCE

August 1973 to present, Gotham Advertising Agency, Chicago, Illinois. Rough-sketch artist and layout person.

September 1970 to August 1973. Freelance children's book illustrator, Chicago, Illinois.

June 1968 to August 1970, Bloom Art Studio, Chicago, Illinois. Responsibilities included artwork through rough layout to finished design for major advertising campaigns for women's beauty-care product line, food manufacturer's customer-use booklets, and a variety of individual illustrations sold to clients. Cartoon style was fully developed during this stage and became my professional signature.

EDUCATION

Rhode Island School of Design, 1966 to 1968. Studied commercial illustration.

Boone Commercial High School, Kansas City, Kansas. Graduated June 1966. Studied vocational course in commercial art.

INTERESTS

Illustrating children's books.

PERSONAL

Single   Born 7-2-48
Will relocate   Good health

*Art director, art production
manager, freelance artist, graphic-
arts salesperson, layout artist*

COMPUTER PROGRAMMER

<u>Nancy Edelman</u>

<u>Computer Programmer</u>

<u>Job Objective</u>

Position as lead programmer with supervisory responsibilities.

<u>Work History</u>

1972-present   Senior programmer. Computron Electronics, Inc.
                Primary task was to convert tabulating and bookkeeping
                systems for three major clients to computer programs
                and to write reports recommending hardware they would
                require.

1967-1972   Programmer. Datatronics, Inc. Four weeks of intensive
                classroom and on-the-job training prepared me to take
                on responsibilities as full-time programmer. Was in-
                volved in creating programs and checking programs of
                others.

<u>Education</u>

1963-1967   B.S., data processing and accounting, Tri-State College.
                Have attended four seminars since graduation to update
                myself on software and new technology.

1959-1963   Green Mountain High School, graduated with honors.

<u>Personal</u>
5187 Arlington Drive
Nashville, Tennessee 37212
Phone: 594-8900
Single; excellent health
Will relocate

References furnished on request.

*Computer operator, computer
programmer, data processor,
keypunch operator, systems analyst*

COPYWRITER

Rowena Dunne

OBJECTIVE

Copywriting position in which I can use my expertise in food marketing.

WORK HISTORY

1972-present   Senior Copywriter, Burton Advertising.
Chief copywriter on five major food accounts, responsible
for two monthly magazines published by clients, one newsletter, and several miscellaneous reports and booklets
geared to the consumer market. Wrote a cookbook for a major
client in 1975.

1970-1972   Copywriter, International Food Advertisers, Inc.
Wrote wide variety of copy for booklets, advertisements, and
brochures describing various food products. Clients included Egg Council and three manufacturers of prepared foods.

1968-1970   Administrative assistant and researcher, Food, Inc., a con-
cern that published three monthly magazines geared to the
food industry. In addition to my secretarial responsibilities, I gradually began to research articles and write
brief pieces for these publications.

EDUCATION

1968, B.A., Blackson University, liberal arts.
1966, associate's degree, Seabrook Junior College, liberal arts.
Have taken various night-school courses:

    Copywriting, Indiana University Extension
    Business Law, Indiana University Extension
    Business Administration and Marketing, Advertiser's Institute
    Marketing Strategies, Advertiser's Institute

PERSONAL

Phone: 888-0907
Married, three children
Health, excellent
139 Seabrook Lane
Oceanview, California 94586

References and samples available on request.

Writer, direct-mail writer, house-
organ editor, press agent,
procedure writer, technical writer

CREDIT MANAGER

CINDY THOMAN
142 Lake Drive
Indianapolis, Indiana 46259
Phone: 472-3381

Job Objective   Position as credit manager of retail clothing store or in department-store credit department.

Personal   Married, one school-age child.
Willing to relocate in any major Midwestern city.

Work Experience

July 1978
to
present

Assistant Credit Manager for XXX Corporation, the credit division of a retail clothing store, located in Lima, Ohio.
Assisted customers in filling out applications for credit, checked credit references, and wrote report regarding granting of credit. Worked closely with credit agencies when customer was under consideration for credit. Reviewed and passed on credit-agency reports. When credit manager took a two-month leave, I assumed responsibility for twelve-person office, managing work of clerks, typists, and bookkeepers.

October 1970
to
June 1978

Trainee in First Federal Bank's program for recent college graduates. Worked various assignments as book-keeper, collection teller, and loan-approval trainee. Promoted in January 1972 to Junior Loan Officer. Major responsibility was to help customers complete applica-tions for loans, check credit references, and report recommendation to board of vice presidents, who made decision about granting loan.

Education   Graduated from University High School, Bloomington, Indiana, June 1966. B.A. from Purdue University, 1970; major, economics; minor, business administration.

Bank branch manager, collection manager, commercial loan officer, financial manager

DENTAL ASSISTANT

DENTAL ASSISTANT

Beth LeBrun
Phone: 763-8974

3488 Stockton Drive
Waverly, New Mexico 87501

JOB OBJECTIVE: Position in dentist's office that includes
public contact and possibly some work in educating the public
to better dental practices. I feel that besides having the
skills necessary to function as a dental assistant, I have
teaching talents that I could contribute to any dentist's practice.

TRAINING: Mount Ryder Junior College, 1970. Awarded certificate in dental assisting. In addition to required courses, I
took typing, office management, and business accounting. High
school graduate, equivalency certificate awarded, 1968.

PROFESSIONAL: Certified as Dental Assistant by Certifying
Board of New Mexico.

WORK EXPERIENCE: Office of John Smithton, D.D.S., 1970 to
present. Responsibilities have included recordkeeping on
patient's health as well as billing, assisting dentist in preparing materials for making impressions and doing restoration
work, and exposing X-ray film. In 1975, I initiated a program
to teach dental hygiene to children. This program, which con-
sists of a fifteen-minute talk using a puppet, has become a
regular part of the office procedure for any patient under the
age of eight. I have fulfilled requests for me to give this
talk to various grade-school classes in the community.

REFERENCES: References and samples of work available on request.

*Dental hygienist, dentist,
paramedic*

DIETITIAN — New Graduate

RESUME

PERSONAL
Marvin Brye
1345 Brilton Lane
Norwich, Connecticut 06360
Phone: 888-8367
Single
Will relocate

EDUCATION
M.S., foods and nutrition, 1979
Cum laude
Connecticut State College

B.S., institutional management, 1977
Connecticut State College

WORK
EXPERIENCE
Internship, Connecticut State Hospital and
  Nursing Home Facility, 1978
Internship was divided into rotating services.
I elected to work in gerontology, patient diet
education, meal service, and outpatient coun-
seling.

For four summers, I also worked at the Connecticut State Nursing Home Facility as a junior
chef and during the last year as a diet counselor.

HONORS
Registered dietitian

PUBLICATIONS
Author of article, "The Role of Education in the
Diet of Persons over Seventy," published in
National Hospital Dietitian.

REFERENCES
References and copy of article available on
request.

Dietitian, nutritionist

PHYSICIAN

George Goodman, M.D.
230 Riverside Drive, New York 10022
Phone: (work) 212-449-8900 (home) 212-666-7830

Job goal: Partnership as pediatrician in small- to medium-sized private clinic or group practice.

Experience: Currently chief resident, Mount Sinai Medical School and Hospital. Worked for one year between internship and residency in emergency ward of Central Appalachia Hospital, about forty miles outside Lexington, Kentucky. My pediatric specialty is neonatology.

1976-1979	Residency
1975-1976	Emergency-room assignment
1973-1975	Internship

Education: 1969-1972, attended medical school, Indiana University, Indianapolis, Indiana. 1968, graduated from Indiana University, Bloomington, Indiana, magna cum laude, in pre-medical studies and chemistry.

Personal: Wish to remain in New York City. Married, with three children.

References available on request.

Dentist, paramedic

DOCTOR'S ASSISTANT

Bernard Wharton
5198 Fifty-fifth Street
Cleveland, Ohio 44122
Phone: 870-3173

Job Objective   Position as doctor's assistant; private or small
                     clinical practice preferred.

Work History   Cleveland City Hospital. 1973-present. Worked as
                     paramedic in emergency, surgery, and psychiatric
                     services. Involved in routine patient care, assisted
                     with medical examinations and minor surgery, dispensed
                     medicine on psychiatric ward, and worked with group
                     therapy.

Education   Cleveland City College, 1971-1973.
                     Paramedical course, included part-time internship at
                     Cleveland City Hospital.
                     Cleveland City High School, 1963-1967.

Military   U.S. Army, 1967-1971. Trained as paramedic. Stationed
                     in Saigon. Honorable discharge with rank of specialist.

References   Furnished on request.

Laboratory technician, paramedic

RESUME OF

EDWARD BISHOP

PERSONAL   Single   400 Drivers Lane
                    Will relocate   Chicago, Illinois
                    Born December 12, 1959   312-355-0056

EDUCATION   Graduated spring 1979 from Industrial Design
                    Institute after completing two-year course in
                    drafting. Awarded associate degree.

                    Graduated spring 1977 from Acton Vocational
                    High School. Took four years each of physical
                    science, drafting, and industrial design.

SUMMER WORK   Worked construction projects for past four
                    summers. Achieved junior rank as carpenter.

JOB OBJECTIVE   Beginner's position in middle-size architectural
                    firm as tracer.

Architect, mechanical artist

ECONOMIST

Joan McElroy   Will relocate
4560 Endview Lane   Will travel
Palo Alto, California 94300
Phone: 405-566-7603

Job Objective

Seeking research position in government agency. Areas of specialty: crop
forecasting, price-wage index evaluation.

Employment History

Blackwell Insurance Agency, Riverside, Montana
October 1971-May 1973
Actuary assistant
Worked primarily as staff statistician, compiling actuarial tables based
on absenteeism.

First Federal Bank, Riverside, Montana
May 1973-present
Statistician
Responsible for ongoing review of wheat-crop forecasts prepared by junior
statisticians. Supervised staff of two.

Education

Graduated from Montana State University
B.A. in public economics; minor in business administration, January 1973

Am currently attending night school. Anticipate receiving master's degree
in economics in June 19__.

Budget analyst, comptroller,
economic analyst, financial analyst,
financial forecaster, statistician

EDITOR

Rosemary Smith
536 Brompton, Apt. 3-S
Chicago, Illinois 60657
Telephone: (Residence) 312/472-3882 (Office) 312/267-6868, Ext. 570

OBJECTIVES

To be a project editor in a college or elementary/high school department.
My major fields of competence and interest are Modern Languages, Education,
Social Sciences, and Humanities.

SUMMARY

I have been an editor in textbook publishing for over ten years. Currently,
I am a project editor at Randolph College Publishing Co., where I am in
charge of coordinating three college-level French projects and am responsible for supervising the personnel involved. These projects are comprised
of ten components: two texts, two readers, two workbooks, two instructor's
manuals, and two sets of tapes. In addition to coordinating and supervising, I am involved in editing, production, and product development. Prior
to being a project editor, I was a manuscript editor at Jackson Publishing
for college-level French, education, and psychology texts. My duties as a
manuscript editor involved copyediting, content editing, production, and
working with designers, artists, authors, and typesetters. I entered
publishing as an editor in the elementary/high school department of Elementary School Plus Publishing Co., where my duties consisted mainly of
writing, rewriting, and doing some production and design work. I have two
years of teaching experience at the eighth- and ninth-grade levels. I have
a Magistere degree in French, an M.A.T. degree in French/Education, and a
B.A. degree in French and music.

EMPLOYMENT HISTORY

Dates	Title	Institution	Location
present-3/76	Project Editor (college)	Randolph College Publishing Co.	New York
2/76-4/73	Manuscript Editor (college)	Randolph College Publishing Co.	New York
3/73-9/69	Editor (el/high)	Elementary School Plus Publishing Co.	New York
6/69-9/67	French Teacher	Easton Junior High School	Watertown, Massachusetts

*Acquisitions editor, freelance editor,
house-organ editor, journalist, junior
editor, photojournalist, senior
editor, trade journalist*

(Continued)

EDUCATION

Dates	School	Location	Major Fields	Degree
9/66-6/67	Sorbonne	Paris, France	French	Magistere (cum laude)
9/65-8/66	Brown University	Providence, R.I.	French/Education	M.A.T.
9/61-6/65	Randolph-Macon Woman's College	Lynchburg, Va.	Music/French	B.A.
9/58-6/61	York Community High School	Elmhurst, Ill.	College Prep.	Diploma

PRODUCT-DEVELOPMENT EXPERIENCE

I have surveyed and analyzed competitive texts, conducted telephone surveys of instructors, solicited written critiques, and prepared guidelines for revision in planning new editions and developing new texts.

SKILLS AND ABILITIES

Editing Skills
copyediting, content editing, writing, rewriting, proofreading, working with authors and sponsoring editors

Production Skills
manuscript markup; page layout; experience with photos, line art, design, audio tapes

Managerial Skills
supervisory skills, budget control, scheduling

Background Abilities
teaching experience, fluency in French

Strong Points
rewriting, selecting visuals, dealing with authors, planning and organizing, meeting deadlines, staying within budgets, getting the best talent involved, shaping books to market needs. The books I edited have sold well.

ENVIRONMENTAL HEALTH INSPECTOR

A. Coleman Noyes II

4077 Coolidge Drive   Phone: 332-1040
Apartment 3
Littleton, Colorado   80120

Job Objective:

Position in environmental control with state or federal agency.

Work History:

Health inspector, Littleton Environmental Agency, 1975-present.
Responsibilities include examining suspected sites of pollution, con-
ducting laboratory tests, collecting routine air and water samples for
monthly testing.

Education:

B.S., University of Colorado, 1975. Environmental health, major;
biology, minor.

Professional:

Licensed by State of Colorado

Personal:

Married, with four children
Will relocate

References:

Available on request.

Public administrator

EXECUTIVE SECRETARY

<u>Executive Secretary</u>

Martina Nunez
746 Cherry Drive
Logansport, Wyoming 82640
387-8455

<u>Work Experience</u>

1975-present. Connors Manufacturing. Secretary to vice president in charge of operations.

1970-1975. Film Masters, Inc. Secretary to executive vice president.

1962-1975. Mathews, Mathews, Targ, and Wolford, Counselors. Secretary to three senior partners in law firm specializing in corporate law.

1961-1962. Starlite Styrofoam Manufacturers, Inc. Responsibilities included general typing and light bookkeeping.

<u>Education</u>

1961. Dyer Secretarial School. Class standing: 4 out of 56.

<u>Skills</u>

Dictaphone
Shorthand--120 w.p.m.
Typing--90 w.p.m.

<u>References</u>

Will be furnished on request.

Administrative secretary, business-machine operator, general office worker, office manager

FILM EDITOR

<u>Resume of</u>

<u>Jacqueline Remstadt</u>

<u>Personal</u>   50 Mountain Laurel Drive
                 San Jose, California 95100
                 Phone: 487-9856 (home); 857-9905 (office)

<u>Work
Experience</u>   <u>Freelance film editor, 1975 until present.</u>

                 Specialty: animation and short documentaries
                 on subjects of interest to children and young
                 adults.

                 <u>Paramount Studio, Hollywood, California,
                 1962-1975.</u> Edited full-length feature films.

                 <u>Independent Photographers' Union, San Jose,
                 California, 1959-1962.</u> Worked as photographer
                 in industrial films; for first year was photog-
                 rapher's assistant.

<u>Education</u>   San Jose Junior College, 1957-1958.
                 Studied under Sam Reilly in film department.

<u>References</u>   Available.

Photographer, photojournalist

57

FREELANCE EDITOR

FREELANCE EDITOR

Brenda Thomas
433 South Lombard Avenue
Oak Park, IL 60302
312-348-0090

Education:

Completing M.A. in anthropology, Roosevelt University

Faculte de Medecin, Universite d'Aix-Marseille, Marseille, France, 1976-1977

B.A. with Honors in Anthropology, Roosevelt University, June 1974

Roosevelt University, Chicago, IL, 1972-1974

Harper College, Palatine, IL, 1970-1972

Skills:

Copyediting, rewriting, proofreading, cookbook editing

Clients:

Copyediting, proofreading-

    Nelson-Hall, Inc., 325 West Jackson, Chicago, IL 60606
    Law in American Society Foundation, 33 North LaSalle,
        Chicago, IL 60602

    Aldine Publishing Co., 529 South Wabash, Chicago, IL 60605

Copywriting-

    Chemical Dynamics Corp., 4554 North Broadway, Chicago, IL 60611

References:

Will be furnished when requested.

Senior editor, copyeditor, house-organ editor, reporter

GEOGRAPHER

Claude Trevor
3080 Eddy Street
Rockeville, Maryland 20014
487-9472

JOB OBJECTIVE

Teaching position with four-year university in geography-ecology department with strong commitment to the field.

CAPSULE HISTORY

For the past five years, I have taught part-time at Northeastern Junior College. I am the only instructor in geography and have organized and developed the three courses I teach: Geography I, Ecology I and Ecology II. In addition, I have held a full-time position as a geographer with the State Department of Environmental Science. I have also worked as a community-development specialist and a site researcher.

CHRONOLOGICAL HISTORY

1974-present   Ecologist, State Department of Environmental Science. Worked in soil and water testing and analysis.

                Taught part-time at Northeastern Junior College.

1972-1974   Community Development Specialist, County Government. Did site research for new developments and for communities planning physical expansion; checked that county criteria for building, plumbing, and electricity installation were met.

1970-1972   G.S. Highon Manufacturing, producer of wood veneers. Worked as site researcher; was primarily responsible for selection of three tentative sites for new plant locations.

EDUCATION

1970   Ph.D., geography and environmental analysis, Western Science University
1967   M.A., environmental science, All-State University
1966   B.A., geography (major), geology (minor), All-State University

PERSONAL

Divorced, no children
Will relocate

References available on request.

Demographer, metallurgist, physicist, professor, zoologist

HOSPITAL ADMINISTRATOR

James Bell
1300 Avenue A
Temple, Texas 76501
Phone: 444-8090

OBJECTIVE   Responsible middle-management position in major urban
                   hospital. I am especially qualified in the area of
                   purchasing and general operations.

CAPSULE   Have worked for fifteen years in all phases of hospital
                   administration and have developed special expertise in
                   cost cutting while maintaining quality.

EXPERIENCE   Assistant department head buyer, purchasing. Assumed
                   variety of responsibilities in all areas of hospital
                   administration. Gathered information and wrote annual
                   budget-planning report.

                   Department assistant, Ladywood Hospital. Worked pri-
                   marily in budgeting and operations. Reduced amounts
                   expended in various supply areas as follows:
                       Linens   12%
                       Utilities   3%
                       Laboratory supplies   20%

EMPLOYMENT   1970-present. Mountainside Hospital, Cloverdale,
HISTORY   California.

                   1970-1963. Ladywood Hospital, Boxton, California.

PUBLICATIONS   Report to AMA titled "Hospital Standards Throughout
                   the United States."
                   HEW report: "Hospital Operations and Middle
                   Management."

PERSONAL   Married.
                   Will relocate.
                   Will travel.

EDUCATION   M.A., 1962, public health, University of Michigan.
                   B.A., 1960, public health and business, Stanford.

REFERENCES   Furnished on request.

Executive, hotel manager,
purchasing agent

HOME ECONOMIST

LOLA BUCHANAN
30 Maple Drive
Dallas, Texas 75206
Phone: 862-1102

JOB OBJECTIVE

A position as a home economist testing new products for a small- to middle-sized firm.

PERSONAL

Will relocate.
Will travel.

WORK HISTORY

1970-1979   Teacher, food chemistry and general home economics, Arlington High School, Kent City, Virginia.

Freelance consultant to three major food firms. Specialized in testing new food products and writing reports suggesting how they might best be marketed.

EDUCATION

1969   Awarded B.S. in home economics. Major: food chemistry. Minor: business administration.

LANGUAGES

1968   Lived and worked in Grenoble, France. Fluent in French. Wrote paper on "Convenience Foods Acceptance in the French Marketplace," accepted for publication in Food Chemistry Journal.

References will be furnished on request.

Dietitian, nutritionist, teacher

INDUSTRIAL ENGINEER

INDUSTRIAL ENGINEER

James Teal
303 Austin Drive
Tulsa, Oklahoma   74101
282-0810

Capsule: Seven years experience as industrial engineer specializing in financial planning and personnel management. Recently passed the examination for state license. Am seeking position with small industrial firm where I can be assured of multiple responsibilities and growth.

Work Chronology: 1975 to present. A.B. Johnston, Inc.
Title: senior industrial engineer. Headed team of eight specializing in financial planning for the firm, which showed a regular annual profit of $10 million. By cutting costs in supplies and personnel, we were able to save the company $1.5 million last year. Part of the year was devoted to an extensive analysis of new products and directions that would be open to the company in the 1980s.

1972 to 1975. Stonecraft Engineering Industries, Inc.
Began as junior engineer working under supervision of department head. In 1973, was appointed assistant to department head. In 1974, when department head retired, was appointed to replace him. I introduced the team study approach, which is still used at the company today.

Education: B.S., engineering, M.I.T., 1972
Full-scholarship student; also worked 30 hours a week for four years during school.

Personal: Married, with three children
Will travel

References: Furnished on request

Chemical engineer, civil engineer, electrical engineer, production manager

62

INTERIOR DECORATOR

RICHARD SAGE

INTERIOR DESIGNER

66 Park Row   Home: 212-348-9613
New York, New York 10017   Office: 212-440-3201

EMPLOYMENT

1970-1979. Sage Antique Exports, Inc., Paris, France.
Owned antique importing business, dealing mostly with 18th- and
19-century furniture. Also imported some fabric. Recently
sold business because of desire to return to U.S.

1961-1970. Fabric designer, Carlton Furniture Co., New York
City. Designed and produced upholstery fabric.

PROFESSIONAL MEMBERSHIPS

American Society of Interior Designers, since 1969.

EDUCATION

B.A., Rhode Island School of Design, interior design and fabric
design.

PERSONAL

Born 4-13-35
U.S. citizen

Business references available on request.

Department-store manager,
furniture salesperson

JEWELER

<u>Andrew Marley</u>

600 West Ninety-ninth Street   212/666-3890
New York, New York   10025

Job Objective

Seeking management responsibilities in small jewelry store with option
to buy.

Employment

1973 to present. Ring repairer and jewelry salesman.
    Radnor Downtown Jewelers, New York City.

1972-1973. Apprentice modelmaker and stonesetter.
    Chilton Jewelry Manufacturing, New York City.

1968-1971. Apprentice program in colored stone setting.
    Excel Jewelry Manufacturers, New York City.

Education

1964-1968. Radnor High School, Radnor, Pennsylvania.

Personal

Married, with three children
Wish to relocate near but outside New York City
Health excellent
Born 1-20-50

References will be furnished on request.

LABOR-RELATIONS NEGOTIATOR

<u>Stanley James</u>

JOB OBJECTIVE

Position with private industry as labor-negotiator.

CAPSULE HISTORY

Nine years experience with local and state government. Specialties include handling of worker grievances, wage-hour compliance, and contract negotiation.

PERSONAL

1300 West Orange Avenue
West Orange, New Jersey 07052
Phones: 555-0987 (home)
         666-3991 (office)
Will relocate; will travel
Married, with two children

WORK HISTORY

<u>New Jersey Wage and Hour Compliance Agency.</u>
My responsibilities included overseeing union-management relations; investigating wage-and-hour complaints; writing reports recommending action on investigation. A large portion of my time with the agency was spent preparing a 450-page report on the status of the state's affirmative-action programs for the Department of Health, Education, and Welfare.

<u>West Orange City Government, Mayor's Labor Relations Office.</u>
Major areas of responsibility and interest included contract negotiations for city workers, union-management relations, daily labor-relations responsibilities, and handling workers' grievances.

CHRONOLOGY

7-16-73 to present.
New Jersey Wage and Hour Compliance Agency

8-1-63 to 7-13-73.
West Orange City Government, Mayor's Labor-Relations Office.

EDUCATION

M.A., industrial relations, Atlanta State College
B.A., political science, U.C.L.A., with honors
Scholarship student

REFERENCES

Furnished on request

*Attorney, minority-rights worker,
wage and salary administrator*

65

LABORATORY TECHNICIAN

Barbara Roth
70999 Mercy Lane
Dubuque, Iowa 52001
Phone: 888-7054

Summary: Nine years of experience, five as an assistant laboratory technician working on measles vaccine, and three years as a technician working on a cancer research project. Have attended various training programs and seminars in the U.S. and Europe; have presented five papers at seminars.

Objective: Seeking position as senior technician in cancer research.

Employment: Honore Laboratories, Inc., Chicago, Illinois. September 1970-October 1975. Assistant laboratory technician. Honore, a major drug-research firm, runs a six-month training program for all new technicians, in which I was a participant. Was then assigned as assistant laboratory technician, working under John Gedding, Ph.D., specialist in vaccine research. Worked on long-term vaccine development.

Chem-Ease Laboratories, Dubuque, Iowa. November 1975-present. Laboratory technician working on cancer research project under supervision of Marya Knightley, Ph.D. Was sent as company representative to four international conferences; presented papers on our cancer project at 1977 and 1978 conferences. Three other papers were presented through my initiative at U.S. Laboratory Technicians for Cancer Research annual meetings.

Education: Purdue University, Ph.D., 1970, oncological research; M.A., 1964, chemistry; B.A., 1962, chemistry.

Bacteriologist, biochemist, biologist, medical technician

LIBRARIAN

Personal

Karl Rozin
422 Martin Street
Stanford, California 94305
Phone: 588-9080

Education

M.A., 1969, U.C.L.A., library science with specialty in acquisitions.
B.A., 1967, San Jose State University, library science.

Languages

Fluent in Spanish; reading knowledge of French and German.

Work Experience

April 1970-present
Assistant librarian, children's department, San Francisco City Library.
Hired to do acquisitions part-time and to develop a summer reading program
for school-age children. Promoted to full librarian, children's department,
June 1976. Supervised a staff of five assistants and did most of the ac-
quisitions work for the children's department.

June 1967-April 1970
General library trainee, San Jose Community Library.
Because library was small, I was able to work in all departments at various
times during my first two years there. In 1969, I was promoted to assistant
children's librarian. Worked to establish interlibrary loan for children's
books. This service has enabled three intercounty libraries to reduce their
acquisitions expenditures by sharing purchases.

Throughout college, I worked as a library assistant in the main university
library.

References

Available on request.

Corporate librarian, school librarian,
supervisor

MANUFACTURING EXECUTIVE

Benjamin Drew
1821 Maple Heights Drive
Wyckoff, New Jersey 07481
Phone: 202-348-0040

OBJECTIVE

A responsible position offering career opportunity, expansion of knowledge, and an immediate challenge. I am particularly qualified to contribute as a general manager or vice president of manufacturing.

GENERAL

Have held a variety of positions, from foreman to engineer, and am currently totally responsible for the manufacturing management and profitability of a three-facility division of a Fortune 500 firm.

AREAS OF EXPERIENCE

PRESENT
Manufacturing Manager: Report to the president; have complete responsibility for three manufacturing plants; approximately $30,000,000 sales; 550 employees.

My first four years in this position produced these gains:

Return on assets	increased	570%
Net earnings	increased	450%
Sales	increased	140%

Significant accomplishments:

Scrap	reduced	15%
Productivity	increased	15%
Shipping expense	reduced	25%
Customer returns	reduced	50%
Compensation claims	reduced	50%
Customer service	reduced delivery slips	80%

The above achievements were due to my expertise in analysis; my securing cooperation, competitiveness, and motivation from all concerned and especially between plants; my setting goals with proper and meaningful measurements; and, most of all, my simultaneous involvement in all areas.

I designed and installed our individual facility machine loading-scheduling system, which increases machine utilization and presents backlog vs. capacity, labor needs vs. payroll, and production slip notification.

I negotiated two multiyear union contracts with annual increases under 6% at our New Jersey plant. (Southern plants are non-union.)

*Business executive, comptroller,
financial analyst, production
supervisor, purchasing manager*

PRIOR
EXPERIENCE

<u>Systems Engineer</u>: I established the manufacturing standards
in all departments in conjunction with the design and imple-
mentation of the standard cost system.

<u>Manager of Information Services</u>: I improved and computerized
the inventory-control system (Burroughs 342). I also re-
designed and converted the sales analysis and the gross
profit systems to the parent corporation's central computer
(Burroughs 3500).

<u>Product Engineer</u>: My adeptness at analyzing and solving
problems quickly resulted in Qualified Product Listings for
all military specifications within our manufacturing capabilities. These included Mil-C-17, Mil-C-915, Mil-W-2194,
and Mil-W-16878, and required both in-depth knowledge of the
characteristics of all available insulating and jacketing
materials and the ability to influence cognizant Government
officials. Because of my broad product knowledge, I was
called into all wire and cable problem areas. I received a
commendation from REA (Rural Electrification Agency),
together with its approval of my version of our company
telephone cable specifications.

<u>Product Manager</u>: I secured complete cooperation and team
effort through my ability to anticipate and provide for the
total needs of the manufacturing operation. My internal
specifications always include step-by-step detail, such as
type, size, and number of fillers to fit into cable inter-
stices; picks/inch on a particular type braiding machine;
reel type and size as dictated by the operation; in-process
and final test requirements and certifications; packing and
shipping instructions, etc. Accurate cost-accounting base,
correct delivery dates, and precise purchasing information
are additional benefits of the complete manufacturing process
sheet.

<u>Sales Engineer</u>. I utilized my analytical and engineering
abilities to coordinate plant capabilities with customer
requirements. I designed the first wires insulated with
"Kapton H Film" (Polyimide) for the Titan missile, and co-
authored a technical paper on these constructions. I also
fashioned the first gas-tight, shielded, silicone rubber
cable for the Con Edison nuclear power station.

(Continued)

<u>Foreman (college, senior year)</u>: I supervised the magnet wire department, comprised of 60 men. Improved employee morale led to fewer union grievances and increased production. This was instrumental in the reinstating of monthly supervisory bonuses.

EMPLOYMENT
HISTORY

4/1968-present   company name by request--engaged in the manufacture of bare and plated electrical conductors.

2/1967-3/1968   Production Manager, Monolith, Inc.

4/1962-1/1967   Product Control Manager, Bable Industries, Inc.

5/1956-3/1962   Cable Engineer, Xenia Products, Inc.

2/1954-2/1956   Acting First Sergeant, Xenia Products, Inc.

1953   Foreman, Xenia Products, Inc.

PERSONAL

Born May 9, 1931, married, two children, excellent health. Enjoy tennis, handball, and bowling. Travel extensively and am willing to relocate.

EDUCATION

Iowa State University, B.S. Industrial Management, 1954
Pace College, Graduate School, 33 credits toward accounting
  M.B.A.
U.S. Army basic electronics and advanced radar schools.

ORGANIZATIONS

American Society for Testing and Materials
National Electrical Manufacturers Association
Society of Automotive Engineers, (A-2H)
  Electrical Wire and Cable Subcommittee

MARKET RESEARCHER

MARKET RESEARCHER

Mindy Pickette
Apartment 2A
Hillside Apartment Complex
Bethesda, Maryland 20014
Phones: 833-8578 (office)
574-1139 (home)

JOB OBJECTIVE

Position as market researcher in food industry, senior analyst level pre-
ferred with supervisory responsibilities.

EMPLOYMENT RECORD

Senior market research analyst, 1971-present
Chem Food Products, Inc. Responsible for testing and development
of five new product lines. Devised several approaches for testing,
did preliminary tests, and wrote recommendations for methods to be
used in mass market tests.

Research assistant, 1968-1971
Cornell University, food research department. Responsible for editing and coding consumer responses, tabulating survey returns, and
reporting on consumer survey findings.

EDUCATION

B.S., marketing, 1967; M.A., business administration, Cornell University,
1968

*Home economist, marketing
manager, marketing sales director,
media analyst, nutritionist,
production manager, statistician*

MERCHANT MARINE OFFICER

Terence Spiegel

Merchant Marine Officer

Personal

130 Western Avenue
Brooklyn, New York 11201
Phone: 857-1487
Born 3-18-50
U.S. citizen
Health: excellent (U.S. Public Health Service Approval)

Job History

SS Argentina, 1974-present
    Second mate, assigned to navigation duties, 1977 to
      present
    Third mate, assigned to signaling equipment and cargo
      supervision, 1974-1977

Education

U.S. Merchant Marine Academy, Kings Point, New York, graduated
  top fifth of class, August 1974

Professional

Member, Brotherhood of Marine Officers

References

Available on request

OFFICE MANAGER

Ann N. Wolf
3520 N. Lake Shore Drive
Chicago, Illinois 60657
312-996-2801

JOB RECORD:

July 1968 - present
PGM, Inc., 640 North LaSalle Street, Chicago (337-7676)
Advertising and sales promotion
Office Manager - Bookkeeper
  Supervised a staff of three.
  Handled corporation books, including payroll, accounts payable and
    receivable, billing.
  Shorthand and typing (IBM Executive).
  Proofread copy for ads, catalogues, sales-promotion pieces.
  Handled group health and life insurance and all other company insurance.
  Heavy telephone and in-person contact with clients and suppliers.
  Composed correspondence.
  Acted as administrative assistant to three corporate officers.

April 1965 - July 1968
Hartwig Exhibitions (no longer in business in Chicago)
Designers and manufacturers of trade-show exhibits
Secretary-Receptionist
  Handled reception and phone.
  Took dictation from four salesmen and production manager.
  Typed on IBM Selectric.
  Handled all phases of office work usually associated with a one-girl
    office.

October 1959 - April 1965
Associated Employers of Illinois, 221 North LaSalle Street, Chicago
Non-profit employers' association
Secretary-Receptionist
  Managed one-girl office.
  Transcribed correspondence from shorthand and dictaphone.
  Acted as receptionist and handled phones.
  Did light bookkeeping, including handling membership dues and payroll.
  Planned luncheon and dinner meetings for association members. This
  included handling seating arrangements and coordination with hotels
  where meetings were held.

Business-machine operator, clerk,
executive secretary, public
administrator, stenographer   (Continued)

Previous jobs included four years as secretary to a sales manager of
Nu Tone, Inc. (no longer located in Chicago). Took heavy shorthand and
also dictaphone. One year with U.S. Army Corps of Engineers as secretary to colonel in charge of supply and procurement division.

EDUCATION:

Foreman High School - general and business courses, graduated.
Wright Junior College - business and fine arts courses, associate degree.
Art Institute of Chicago - one year.

Personal references will be supplied if requested.

PARALEGAL

Susan Goldman   Phone: 212-688-7359

<u>Job Objective</u>: Position with full-time paralegal responsi-
bilities in large law firm in New York area.

<u>Work experience</u>:

1977 to present, secretary-paralegal for Dixon & Dixon, New
York. My position, which began as secretary, has gradually
become full-time paralegal. I spend approximately three days
a week in court, and am familiar with the local, state, and
federal court system.

<u>Education</u>:

1977 to present, attending New York University Law School,
evening division.

1972-1976, New York University. B.A., political science.

<u>Personal</u>:

Reside at 340 West Twenty-third Street
New York, New York 10002

<u>References available on request.</u>

Legal secretary, court reporter,
office assistant

PERSONNEL EXECUTIVE

Ruth Ebstein

1800 Terrace Row
Baltimore, Maryland 21200

Home: 888-0912

OBJECTIVE: Key personnel position with a progressive and innovative organization.

SUMMARY: Innovative personnel executive with in-depth knowledge of the profession. Proficient in organization and manpower planning, executive recruiting, wage and salary administration, EEO/Affirmative Action, benefit and pension administration, ERISA compliance, program development, employee and labor relations, operating and fringe-benefit budgeting.

EXPERIENCE: Established personnel department and developed it into a contributing force in management operations.

<u>Personnel Management</u> Conducted organization analysis and structure, manpower planning and development to provide the corporation with efficient human resources.

Increased productivity of professional employees by developing and administering extensive and ongoing management-by-objectives program.

Maintained uninterrupted operations, sustaining trained manpower during several plant and office relocations.

Developed preventive medical program to ensure the health and safety of employees. Minimized lost time and reduced insurance premiums.

<u>Recruitment</u> Reduced employment costs, accomplished more timely placements, and improved caliber of new personnel.

Heavy direct search and selection of managerial, professional, and technical personnel.

Established and maintained effective college recruitment program.

Customer relations employment counselor, minority-rights worker, wage and salary administrator

<u>Wage and Salary</u>	Implemented and directed wage and salary programs. (Hay and factor comparison.)
	Improved and maintained incentive and indirect compensation plans.
<u>Government Relations</u>	Reduced exposure to compliance reviews, individual and class-action suits by designing, directing, and implementing EEO/Affirmative Action plans.
	Ensured compliance with the regulatory agencies and labor laws, keeping all levels of management aware of corporate and individual responsibilities.
<u>Benefits</u>	Managed corporate benefit program covering pensions, insured benefits, and company-sponsored programs.
<u>Communications</u>	Contributed to employee understanding of company's business objectives, functions, policies, and guidelines through direction of employee communication and publication program.
<u>Labor and Employee Relations</u>	Strengthened non-union environment by organizing effective labor and employee-relations program in highly organized industry.
	Developed and implemented numerous support programs and policies in communications, management awareness, supervisory training, labor negotiations, employee relations, health and safety.
<u>Training and Development</u>	Enhanced efficiency by improving supervisor/employee rapport through the development of training programs and operating procedures.
	Identified training and development needs of individuals and groups and implemented programs to meet those needs.
	Conducted in-house management seminars to provide knowledge and understanding over a broad spectrum of subjects.
<u>EDUCATION:</u>	B.S., Indiana University, Psychology/Economics, 1955 Numerous business courses at various organizations and institutions.

(Continued)

77

AFFILIATIONS: Eldorado, Inc.   Director of Personnel
              2/1974-present

              Air Transport Industries   Director of Personnel
              12/71-2/74
              9/59-12/71   Corporate Personnel
                                                 Manager, Director of
                                                 Wage and Salary

PERSONAL: Married, four children
              Will travel/relocate

PROFESSIONAL American Association of Personnel Administrators
ASSOCIATIONS: New York Personnel Managers Association
              Northern New Jersey Employers Association
              American Compensation Society
              Board of Directors, New Jersey Industrial
              Nurses Association

PHARMACIST

R E S U M E

O F

SOLOMON DIDIER   REGISTERED PHARMACIST
1300 Drivers Lane   Married
Oak Point, Michigan 48237   Will relocate
857-1126 (home)   396-1000 (office)

Objective: Assistant manager's position with large drugstore chain.

Work   1974-present, assistant night manager, Total Drugstores, Inc.
Experience: Supervise three registered pharmacists in this all-night
                  drugstore; fill prescriptions, monitor and reorder supplies,
                  and supervise point-of-purchase advertising for three major
                  display counters.

                  1972-1974, pharmaceutical salesperson. Orgon Pharmaceutical
                  Supplies, Inc., Indianapolis, Indiana. Covered Indiana,
                  Ohio, and northern Michigan. Did some test marketing of new
                  product lines in northern Indiana; this entailed introducing
                  productions to potential customers and writing reports indi-
                  cating their responses.

Education: Master's of Pharmacy, Southern Indiana State University,
                  1972. Magna cum laude. (Bachelors and masters program were
                  combined into one five-year curriculum.)

Professional   Licensed to practice pharmacy in Illinois, Indiana, and
Information: Ohio.

References: Will be pleased to furnish on request.

Biochemist, technical salesperson

PHOTOGRAPHER'S STYLIST

PHOTOGRAPHY STYLIST

Anne Porter
134 West Ninety-second
New York, New York 10025
Phone: 212-497-2000

GOAL

To work for innovative, active photographer who can and is willing to use
my varied talents.

CAPSULE EXPERIENCE

I have worked as a stylist for five years. Tasks have ranged from locating
an extremely rare antique and negotiating its rental to sewing costumes and
building room-size sets for use as photo props. I have functioned as office
manager and purchasing agent in addition to stylist and would be willing to
handle these responsibilities again.

WORK CHRONOLOGY

October 1974 to present. Chief stylist and office manager for Taber Greene,
photographer specializing in interior and product shots. Supervised secretary, bookkeeper, and receptionist, while assuming major responsibility for
all styling. When necessary, I hired additional persons to help with set
and prop preparation and supervised their work.

August 1973-October 1974. Window dresser, Mann Department Store.

June 1971-August 1973. Girl Friday for fashion photographer. Booked and
helped select models, bought photography supplies, and kept books for
business in addition to secretarial responsibilities.

EDUCATION

B.A., fine arts, Georgia State University, January 1971.

LANGUAGES

Fluent in French.

INTERESTS

Travel, art, reading.

REFERENCES

Furnished on request.

*Photographer, photographer's
assistant, set designer*

80

PHYSICAL THERAPIST

BETH ANN NELSON

JOB OBJECTIVE

Position as physical therapist that allows a lot of patient contact, preferably with children. Interested in planning and developing physical-therapy programs in addition to administering them.

PERSONAL

Single; excellent health; will relocate; will travel
Reside at 15 Country Club Plaza, Kansas City, Kansas 64108
Phone: 317-350-1042, Extension 330.

PROFESSIONAL

Licensed to practice physical therapy by State of Kansas.

EMPLOYMENT

1974-1979, physical therapist, Dwayne Hospital.
Perform and interpret diagnostic tests and write programs for individual therapy, which are then carried out by staff therapist. Check after six and twelve weeks to make any needed adjustments in programs.

1973-1974, physical therapist, Rehabilitation Center.
Worked part-time while attending school. Assisted therapists with swimming therapy.

EDUCATION

B.A., physical therapy, January 1974, Utah Western University.
B.A., physical education, June 1973, Utah Western University.
Have completed nine hours toward master's in physical therapy.

References on request.

Occupational therapist, nurse, paramedic

PLANT MANAGER

Resume of

Ralph Brunton

122 Western Street

Detroit, Michigan 48200

Phone: 344-0900

Job Objective

Plant manager in medium to large manufacturing company.

Work Experience

<u>1960-Present, ABC Manufacturing Parts Company</u>. Hired as assistant to plant manager on night shift, where I worked for three years. Promoted to assistant to plant manager on day shift in 1972. Became plant manager in 1973. Reorganized work schedules to permit 4 1/2-day work week at same level of productivity and introduced swing shift as an option for workers who desired it.

1955-1960, DEF Motor Company. Assembly-line worker. Served as union representative for three years.

Education

1958-1960. Attended junior college, taking accounting and business-math courses.

1958, graduated from Lane Vocational High School, Detroit, Michigan.

Special Achievements

As union representative, I assisted in contract negotiations on three occasions. As company representative, I attended a seminar on plant managers and labor relations organized by the U.S. Department of Labor. I have developed a specialty in labor relations that I feel would contribute to my ability to run a plant efficiently.

Foreman, mailroom supervisor,
production manager, supervisor

PRODUCT MANAGER

<u>Roberta Wells</u>

1300 Wilson Avenue
St. Louis, Missouri   63119
Phone: 487-4855

<u>Job Objective</u>

Position as designer of women's apparel

<u>Employment History</u>

Junior House Designs, Ltd., 1976-1979

   <u>Trainee</u>. Worked as a sample maker, pattern maker, cutter, and
machine operator.

   <u>Assistant product manager</u>. Responsibilities included estimating
production costs, scheduling work flow, hiring and training new workers,
controlling quality, supervising overall production activities, some
bookkeeping.

<u>Education</u>

Rhode Island School of Design, 1972-1976

   Scholarship student
   Awarded Golden Ace Student Design Award
   Design, major; business administration, minor

<u>Personal</u>

Married, with one child
Will relocate; will travel

References and samples available on request.

*Buyer, clothes designer, fashion
coordinator, inventory-control
administrator, production
supervisor, purchasing agent*

PROFESSIONAL HOUSEKEEPER

Paula Birnbaum
1822 Tinkers Row
Columbus, Ohio   44020
Phone: 399-0010

Single
No children
Will travel
Will relocate

JOB TITLE

Professional housekeeper

EMPLOYMENT RECORD

January 1976-
present

Assistant Buyer, paper and linen supplies.
Bedside Inn Motels, Inc. Sunnybrook Vale, Idaho.
Assisted in buying paper supplies for thirty hotels
in five-state area. Arranged delivery times and
coordinated deliveries. Promoted to department
buyer for linens.

August 1973-
January 1976

Assistant housekeeper, XYZ Hotel, Los Angeles,
California. Originally supervised staff of twenty
who bought linen and paper supplies. Promoted to
buyer for kitchen supplies. Supervised buying staff
of twenty-three. XYZ is a 350-room hotel geared
mostly to convention and summer-vacation business.

EDUCATION AND PROFESSIONAL HONORS

Certified member of National Executive Housekeeping Association.

Graduate, Oakdale High School, Los Angeles, California, top third of
class, 1973.

Have taken the following courses in night school:

Business math I and II
Hotel management I-IV

Inventory-control administrator,
purchasing agent

PSYCHIATRIC NURSE

<u>RESUME</u>

Madeleine Taylor

<u>PERSONAL</u>

Date of Birth: May 27, 1951
Place of Birth: Chicago, Illinois
Correspondence Apt. 2002
Address: 4343 North Clarendon Avenue
Chicago, Illinois 60613
Phone: (312) 281-6296 Home
(312) 975-5101 Work
License Number: 41-141739

<u>EDUCATION</u>

May 1979 M.S.N., St. Xavier College, Chicago, Illinois
August 1976 B.S.N., University of Rhode Island
June 1972 Diploma, Michael Reese Hospital and Medical Center
School of Nursing, Chicago, Illinois

<u>PROFESSIONAL BACKGROUND</u>

1978-79 Clinical Internship; intakes, super-   Community Mental
vised individual, marital, family,   Health Clinic
and group psychotherapy   St. Joseph Hospital
                                          Chicago, Illinois

1978 Clinical Internship; intakes, super-   Mental Health Clinic
vised individual and family psycho-   Grant Hospital
therapy   Chicago, Illinois

1976-present Clinical Nursing Instructor and   Augustana Hospital
Coordinator, Nursing I; clinical and   School of Nursing
classroom instruction.   Chicago, Illinois
Coordinator, Nursing II (psychiatric
nursing).

1975-76 Psychiatric Nurse Clinician; evalua-   Mental Health Clinic
tion of outpatients with emotional   Day-Kimball Hospital
problems, supervision of individual   Putnam, Connecticut
psychotherapy and patient management,
psychiatric consultation to medical-
surgical units

*Hospital administrator, nurse,
psychologist, social worker*

(Continued)

1975	Staff Nurse in alcoholic treatment center; care of the alcoholic during the initial drying-out period and involvement in rehabilitation	Starlight Farms, Inc. Stonington, Connecticut
1974	Assistant Head Nurse; supervision and administration, in-service education, and individual therapy	Illinois State Psychiatric Institute, Chicago, Illinois
1972-74	Staff Nurse; milieu therapy, group therapy, and patient-care planning and treatment	Illinois State Psychiatric Institute Chicago, Illinois
1972	Staff Nurse; primary nursing care on a cardio-vascular thoracic surgical unit	University of Chicago Hospitals and Clinics Chicago, Illinois

PAPERS AND PUBLICATIONS

"The Nurse as a Psychotherapist," submitted for publication to Psychotherapy: Theory, Research and Practice.
"The Nurse as a Psychiatric Consultant." In preparation.

PUBLIC RELATIONS EXECUTIVE

Judith Golden
1600 Main Street
Wilmington, New York 12997
Phone: 860-3123

PERSONAL

Single
Will travel
Will relocate

OBJECTIVE

Managerial position with major corporation in public relations department; would prefer to work with products rather than services.

EMPLOYMENT
7/74-
present

Vice president, Allied Public Relations, Ltd. Supervise staff of three writers. Work with suppliers to buy graphic arts outside firm. Major responsibilities include planning annual public relations activities for five clients, whose products range from tissue paper to school supplies to collectors' plates.

4/72-
7/74

Account executive. Responsibilities were basically the same; I brought the five aforementioned clients to the firm.

1/69-
4/72

Executive secretary to president. Besides regular responsibilities, I started and was responsible for an internal employees' newsletter, which is still being published.

4/68-
1/69

Volunteer director, New Careers for Divorced Women. In addition to handling overall administrative responsibilities, I supervised a volunteer staff of twenty part-timers. A major part of my time was spent organizing and assigning projects and checking to make sure they were completed by the target date. Close supervision was necessitated by the restrictions of working with a part-time staff. Wrote grant proposals that brought our organization $450,000 in federal and state monies, an increase of $300,000 over previous years. Wrote and did production work on series of twenty booklets designed to show divorced women how to re-enter the job market.

EDUCATION

B.S., home economics, Oregon State University, 1954, graduated with honors. Class standing: 2 out of 350.

REFERENCES

Will be furnished on request.

House-organ editor, management consultant, media director, media trainee, press agent

PURCHASING AGENT

SAM NUSBAUM   PURCHASING AGENT

430 Liberty Drive
Apartment 1900
Boston, Massachusetts 02151
Phone: 857-9375

WORK HISTORY

Assistant Buyer   1975-present
M & N Engineering Corporation, Boston, Massachusetts
Responsible for buying technical-division supplies; budget allowed is
$4 million annually.

Junior purchasing agent   1971-1975
Technical Supplies, Inc., Boston, Massachusetts
Began with very comprehensive training program that included three months
in storekeeper's section and three months in buying. After four-month
trial period in buying, assumed responsibility for buying standard office
supplies. In 1974, was promoted to assistant buyer for laboratory supplies
and given responsibility for a $2 million budget.

EDUCATION

M.A., Indiana University, business, 1971
B.A., Purdue University, business management and computer science, 1970
Have attended seminars and taken two post-graduate courses in purchasing
to increase expertise in my field.

PROFESSIONAL HONORS

Applied for Certified Purchasing Manager, awarded by National Association
of Purchasing Management; approval pending, expected in spring 1979.

*Management trainee, purchasing
manager, sales promoter*

REAL ESTATE BROKER

REAL ESTATE BROKER

Janet Jayson

589 Indigo Drive
West Lafayette, Indiana 47906
Phone: 317-857-9486

Experience

1975-present   Aaron Realty, Inc. During the years I have
worked for this company, I have generated
$3 million in home sales. In 1978, I was
named "Best Realtor" for a five-state region.
I am licensed by the State of Indiana.

Education

1950-1954   Round Hill Teachers' College, Round Hill,
North Carolina. B.A., elementary education.

Personal

From 1954 until 1975, I reared three children, was active in
many community organizations and substituted in the elementary
school system approximately 100 days per year. My children
are now college age, and I am looking for full-time, permanent
employment.

Willing to travel. References on request.

*Real estate sales manager, real
estate salesperson, returning
housewife*

RECEPTIONIST

Georgina Martin

190 Austin Drive
Apartment 313
Shawnee Mission, Kansas 66205
Phone: 384-4817

Employment

August 1977-present

Part-time receptionist for
Rollins Textbook Publishers.

January 1975-August 1977

Full-time receptionist for
Edison, Inc., manufacturing firm
with 220 employees. Filled in
on CENTREX switchboard.

Education

1977-present

Part-time student at Trenton
Community College, working on
B.A. in business administration.

References available.

*General office worker, hospital
receptionist, stenographer, typist*

RESTAURANT MANAGER

JOHN ANDERSON

1700 Oneida Drive
499-1944 (office)

Monterey, California 93940
456-1134 (home)

WORK EXPERIENCE

<u>Assistant restaurant manager</u>, Skyline Grill, Skyline City, California.
May 1973 to present. This restaurant is known for the elegance of its
table settings and food presentation, as well as the excellence of its
kitchen. My responsibilities include working closely with the head chef,
ordering food and planning menus, supervising a staff of fifty-five,
ordering all supplies, general budgeting, and maintaining payroll records.

<u>Assistant restaurant manager and host</u>, ABC Restaurants, Inc., Norfolk,
Virginia. May 1971-May 1973.

<u>Short-order chef</u>, ABC Restaurants, Inc., at main store, located in
Louisville, Kentucky. January 1973-May 1973.

EDUCATION

Dexter Junior College, Dexter, Kentucky, awarded associate degree in
restaurant management, June 1973.

Dexter High School, Dexter, Kentucky, graduated January 1971.

PERSONAL

Married; will relocate.

*Chef, food-services worker, hotel
manager, purchasing agent,
purchasing manager*

RETAIL CLOTHING BUYER

Stephen Lieberman
800 Central Park West, Apt. 12
New York, New York 10022
948-9487 (evenings)
857-9487 (daytime)

Summary

Six years' experience in retail clothing, specializing in women's wear. Committed to field and seeking position that offers greater responsibility, more challenge, and room for growth.

Employment History

Buyer, Mini-sette Clothes, Inc., 1974-present
Supervision of sales staff of fifteen; checking invoices of materials received; working with point-of-sale computer terminals to keep up-to-the-minute sales records; writing quarterly report evaluating sales and projecting sales for next quarter.

Buyer Trainee, Juniorettes, Inc., 1972-1974
Worked one month each in sales, stock, reorder, and bookkeeping. After training, I worked as a salesperson while assisting with buying. Responsible for coordinating the fall and spring sales catalogues; worked closely with copywriters and art department.

Education

B.A., Boston State University School of Design, business marketing, 1972. Curriculum included a three-month internship in local department store; afterward I worked in the store as part-time sales help.

Graduated from Boston Central High School, 1968.

Personal

Will travel; will relocate.

References

Available on request.

Buyer trainee, department store manager, estimator, manufacturer's representative, retail-store manager, sales promoter, wholesale clothing buyer

RETAIL FOOD BUYER

RESUME OF

REBECCA SWAIN

1400 Round Hill Drive   Phone: 398-2464
Indianapolis, Indiana   46200

Job Objective:

Challenging position in food management with growth-oriented company.

Work History:

Assistant store manager, Roberts Groceries, Inc.
March 1977 to present
Responsibilities included working in all phases of store management and
coordinating store activities; on several occasions, I filled in for
store manager for two-week periods. Supervised staff of fifty-five.

Salesperson, ABC Canned Foods Supplies, Inc.
September 1975 to February 1977
Traveled in three-state area selling canned foods products lines to
grocery stores. Increased business overall by 250 percent, and picked
up approximately twenty new customers.

Store management trainee, Roberts Groceries, Inc.
July 1974 to September 1975
Six-month training program introduced me to all facets of in-store food
management as well as warehousing, transportation, and accounting. After
training program, I worked in purchasing for six months.

Education:

B.S., Cornell University; major, food management; minor, computer science

Have taken Cornell home-study courses in food distribution, security, and
    food transportation.

*Estimator, food-services worker,
home economist, manufacturer's
representative, purchasing agent,
supermarket manager*

RETAIL SALESPERSON

RETAIL   SALESPERSON

John Waverly
1890 Tiverton Lane
Milwaukee, Wisconsin   53207
Phone: 866-0330

OBJECTIVE   Retail furniture buyer

EXPERIENCE

September 1959   Senior furniture buyer for ABC Department Store in
to Present   Milwaukee. Responsible for all buying of upholstered
                     furniture. Traveled four times a year to regional
                     distributor shows and bought in-store from sales-
                     persons who handled our account. Responsible for
                     monitoring stock and reordering.

July 1948   Employed in various capacities in Milwaukee department
to August 1959   store, the Emporium. Began as sales trainee and was
                     gradually assigned to all departments in addition to
                     working exchange counter. In 1950, became a full-
                     time salesperson in housewares. In 1952, became
                     assistant buyer in housewares.

                     In 1955, promoted to salesperson in furniture depart-
                     ment, where I began working on commission. My commis-
                     sions averaged about 20 percent higher than average,
                     and I estimate that my efforts increased sales in
                     department by approximately $80,000 per year.

                     In 1957, became assistant buyer of furniture.

EDUCATION

1954   Awarded associate degree from junior community college

1945   Graduated from Milwaukee Central High School

MILITARY

1945 to 1948   U.S. Navy, intelligence

1948 to 1954   U.S. Navy Reserves

PERSONAL   Married twenty-two years; three children.

*Furniture salesperson, retail sales
clerk, retail store manager*

SALES REPRESENTATIVE

MICHAEL JAMIESON
1458 North Cleveland
Chicago, Illinois 60640
Phone: 312/858-9201

JOB OBJECTIVE

Position in sales management with innovative textbook company.

WORK HISTORY

<u>Sales representative</u>, Alton Social Science Publisher, 1975 - present.
Covered all Midwest with exception of Chicago. Sold forty-five-book line
that spanned three disciplines. Profits for the territory I covered
increased by the following amounts:

10%, 1975; 28%, 1976; 44%, 1977.

<u>Sales representative</u>, Education Books, Inc., 1974 - 1975.
Responsible for five-state territory in South. Sold thirty books spanning
two disciplines, plus two multimedia kits. Profits in my territory jumped
28% over previous year.

EDUCATION

Boston University, 1974
B.A., English literature and business administration

PERSONAL

Birth date: 7-20-56

Health: Excellent

Willing to relocate

Willing to travel

REFERENCES

Furnished on request

*Manufacturer's representative,
publishing trainee, technical
salesperson*

SOCIOLOGIST

JANETTE TRAYNOR

14 Knightbridge Road
Apartment 12
Alexandria, Virginia   22305
Phones: 202-555-9481 (home)
         202-347-1160 (office)

EMPLOYMENT

1972-present   Research analyst, Department of Health, Education, and
                      Welfare. Interpreted statistics for ongoing project
                      on health of school-age children in Appalachia; par-
                      ticipated in writing 600-page summary report. Other
                      projects included analyzing statistics on food value
                      in school lunch, rising cholesterol levels in children
                      under ten, and snack habits of school-age children

1973-1974   Freelance consultant to Tri-Town Family Counseling
                      Center. Did group and individual counseling with
                      emotionally disturbed children.

EDUCATION

1969-1972   Tri-State Southern University, Ph.D., ethnic studies
                      and race relations

1968-1969   Marymount Women's University, M.A., urban sociology

1964-1968   Marymount Women's University, B.A., sociology

PERSONAL

                      Single, with two children
                      Will relocate

REFERENCES

                      On request

*Caseworker, counselor, family
counselor, job guidance counselor,
medical social worker, occupational
therapist, medical social worker,
police officer, psychologist, social
worker*

96

SPEECH THERAPIST

LOUISE WHEATLEY—SPEECH THERAPIST

PERSONAL
Born 4-11-49
Married, with three children
Health: excellent

487 Round Oak Drive
Providence, Rhode Island 02903
465-7900 (home)

WORK HISTORY

April 1975-
present

Area school therapist. Round Oak County School System.
Primary responsibilities include supervising six other
workers in the three-school area; counseling therapists
as they plan individual therapy for their patients; in-
terpreting test materials for individuals with speech
problems; and routinely testing all first-, third-, and
sixth-graders annually. Develop and conduct group speech
therapy: same age groups of six children work together
for an hour each week. For children who have been pro-
gressing slowly, the results are better than in individual
therapy.

June 1973-
April 1975

Speech rehabilitation therapist. Dixon Rehabilitation
Clinic. Worked with persons suffering from brain damage
and speech impairments that were not birth-related.
Planned and carried out individual therapy.

PROFESSIONAL MEMBERSHIPS AND HONORS

Certified to teach in State of Rhode Island
Certificate of Clinical Competence (Speech)

PUBLICATIONS

"Group Speech Therapy for Grade Schoolers," published May 1977 in
Speech Therapist.
"Group Therapy for Problem Speakers," published August 1977 in Speech
and Hearing Therapist.

EDUCATION

M.A., Purdue University, clinical speech therapy
B.A., Minnesota State University, education and speech pathology
Scholarship student and worked part-time throughout school

Occupational therapist, psychologist,
sociologist

STOCKBROKER

Stock-Market Analyst

Ann Warren

50 East Park Avenue
Louisville, Kentucky 94229
Phone: 502-487-7465 (home)
        502-444-8700, ext. 40

Employment History

1969-
present

Holmes, Inc., a medium-size brokerage firm. Senior vice president. Managed portfolios for fifty clients and supervised a group of five brokers. Group specialized in mutual funds and medical and pharmaceutical stocks.

1965-
1969

Viking & Viking, Stockbrokers, Inc. Market analyst. Worked in a group of eight persons. Responsible for monitoring market activity in three major industries.

1961-
1964

Viking & Viking, Stockbrokers, Inc. Secretary to president for two years. Attended training program in market analysis for one year.

Education

1958-
1961

Kentucky State University. Business major. Graduated with honors. Extracurricular activities included being editor of the business magazine (The New Business Mind) and treasurer of a sorority.

Personal

Single
Willing to relocate
Will travel

References

Available on request.

*Business executive, financial analyst,
investment analyst, portfolio analyst*

TEACHER

ELEMENTARY SCHOOL TEACHER

Dorothy Donberg
440 Melrose
Chicago, Illinois 60657
Phone: 312-558-4700

WORK EXPERIENCE

1974-present   Rockport Elementary School, third-grade teacher.

1973   Rockport Elementary School, special-education teacher. Developed program for bilingual students in Spanish.

EDUCATION

1968-1972   Northern Illinois Teachers' College. Graduated magna cum laude.

Present   Have accumulated nine hours for master's in public school administration and expect to complete degree in 1980.

EXTRACURRICULAR ACTIVITY

1973   Presented paper, "The Bilingual Child in the Chicago School System," at Chicago Regional Teachers' Conference.

PERSONAL

Single; will relocate.

References on request.

TECHNICAL WRITER

SUZANNE BECKETT

Goal

Position as technical writer in private sector where I can use my
expertise and experience in agricultural research.

Work experience

1970-present. Technical writer, Atlantis Oil Co.
Responsible for all stages of preparation of field-use manuals and
fund-request reports. Occasionally write articles for company publication.

1965-1970. Research assistant, Department of Agriculture.
From 1967, also served as associate editor of newsletter directed to
oil industry.

Educational background

B.A., agricultural science (major), journalism (minor), Johnson
Valley College, 1960

Military service

Served two years in WACS. Stationed in Germany. Honorably discharged
with rank of captain. Contributed to Western European U.S. Army newspaper published in Germany, and also worked as technical writer on
medical projects.

Skills

Good at organizing and simplifying complex material
Research
Writing
Familiar with computers and their use in research

Personal

2799 Davenport Drive
Tulsa, Oklahoma 74101
Phone: 232-1970

References available on request
Will relocate

*Direct-mail writer, journalist,
reporter, researcher, writer*

TELEPHONE REPAIRPERSON

MARLENE MARKSON

Personal

487 Sixth Avenue
Arlington, Virginia 22202
Phone: 487-8843

Single
Health excellent
Vision excellent

Job Objective

Position with supervisory responsibilities with independently owned
telephone company.

Work History

1973 to present. PBX installer, employed by Virginia Independent
     Utilities, Inc., a medium-sized telephone company serving twenty-
     county area. Primary responsibility has been installation and upkeep
     on PBX system, but I am trained to install and maintain CENTREX
     system.

Education

1972, graduated from Arlington County Consolidated High School.
1973, vocational training in PBX and CENTREX systems at Virginia Bell
     Technical Training Center.

References

Available on request

Electrical engineer, electrician

TRAVEL AGENT

MARY McCABE — TRAVEL AGENT

JOB OBJECTIVE

Having recently become a certified travel agent in Illinois, I am seeking a position planning international travel with a medium- to large-sized agency.

WORK HISTORY

1975-present   <u>Ticketing agent</u>. Europa Travel Agency, Chicago.

1972-1975   <u>Secretary</u>. Flyaway Travel Agency. After one year, I began to assist agents booking domestic and international flights.

TRAVEL EXPERIENCE

Have traveled to U.S.S.R., Mexico, Western and Eastern Europe—thirty-five countries. Lived in Paris, France, for six months and in Aix-en-Provence for four months.

LANGUAGES

Fluent in French and German

EDUCATION

1971   Graduated, Altamont High School
          Honor Society, cheerleader (three years)

1972   Attended Eastern Women's College, studied French

PERSONAL

500 Michigan Terrace
Chicago, Illinois 60606
Phone: 312/444-0800

References available on request.

Airline reservationist, linguist, reservationist

TYPESETTING SHOP MANAGER

R E S U M E

Paul Petri

1236 West Eddy Street
Chicago, Illinois 60657
312 472 8352

Birth Date:
January 16, 1946

WORK EXPERIENCE

12/76 to present: Adopt, Inc. Manager, Composition Services. I organized the art production department, which was formed by a large Chicago commercial printer to provide it with non-union support services. Under my supervision, this department has grown from a one-person, one-machine operation to an efficient six-person, two-shift shop. All routines, protocols, and standards for the production of type were instituted by me.

11/74 to 12/76: United Press Midwest (financial printing). Planner/Proofreader/Typesetter. Supervised job flow in a twenty-person composing room, computerized pagination and mark-up of indentures, debentures, and most other types of legal and financial documents to conform to SEC standards. Acted as assistant to manager.

9/73 to 11/74: Nurses Association of America. Editorial Assistant and Writer. I held two positions. First, as an editorial assistant on a bimonthly medical journal, I was involved with manuscript production, correspondence, and minute-taking. Second, as an editorial writer for the Committee on Functions and Standards, I organized, edited, and rewrote the work of a committee of nursing professionals formed to define the legal role of OB-GYN-Neonatal nurse practitioners.

10/72 to 8/73: S. Simon Publishing Company. Manuscript Coder. Coded and typeset copy for the trade and educational divisions.

12/70 to 5/72: Credit Information Corporation of Chicago. Credit Information Reporter. On-line terminal operator for computerized credit reporting system (part time).

9/68 to 9/70: Chicago Speakers Council. Director of Speakers Bureau. Worked to obtain speakers on a wide range of topics related to U.S. foreign policy for colleges, clubs, business groups, and educational organizations.

5/68 to 9/68: A.A.A. Corporation (Point Barrow Naval Arctic Research Site). Administrative Assistant. Duties were directly related to the fulfillment of documentation standards set by a Government-maintenance contract that the company held.

Advertising traffic manager, management trainee, offset machine operator, printer, production manager

(Continued)

EDUCATION

9/65 to 5/67: La Universidad de las Americas (Pueblo, Mexico). Liberal arts curriculum with a major in creative writing. Worked for school administration to meet tuition expenses.

6/64: Graduated from Lyons Township High School, La Grange, Illinois.

SKILLS

Budget management, computerized pagination, editorial, mark-up, paste-up, proofreading, Spanish, supervision, type production. Good supervisory skills.

UNDERWRITER

LINDA FOGARTY

JOB OBJECTIVE   Position as underwriter in small- to middle-size insurance
company. Seeking job that will offer growth to managerial
responsibilities.

WORK
EXPERIENCE
   Hilton Insurance Agencies United, Inc.
Underwriter, 1976 to present
Senior claims representative, 1974-1976
My special area of expertise is in major medical policies;
I have a good mastery of medical terminology.

Downing Insurance Company, Inc.
Junior claims representative, 1973-1974
I began in the training program and was advanced to handling
my own claims after six weeks.

Hedrick and Sons, Counselors
Legal secretary, 1972-1973
My work as a legal secretary to three lawyers who specialized
in insurance claims awakened my interest in the insurance
business; it also afforded me an opportunity to become thor-
oughly familiar with the legal terms related to insurance
work.

EDUCATION   B.A., liberal arts, Iowa State University, 1972. Major,
literature; minor, business and management
Graduated from Iowa City High School, 1968

PERSONAL   9487 Shiveley Lane
Elkhart, Indiana 46514
Phone: 948-0397
Will travel, will relocate
Single, good health

*Insurance-claims specialist, wage
and salary administrator*

UNIVERSITY ADMINISTRATOR

RESUME

ALAN GLEN
30 Russian Hill
Apartment 3R
San Francisco, California 94102
Telephone: 280-2843

PROFESSIONAL INTERESTS

Operations and budget management
Research, analysis, and policy determination in higher education.

WORK EXPERIENCE

1972-present: Assistant Vice President, Northern California University
Senior staff officer to Executive Vice President for Administration
Extensive responsibilities in operations management (buildings and grounds,
   administrative services, budget management)
Direct supervision of Office of Publications and Printing
Analyze budget submissions, prepare reports, draft 90% of correspondence
   from office of Executive Vice President
Liaison with purchasing, construction, buildings and grounds, personnel
   management, other support functions
Acting Equal Opportunity and affirmative-action officer (since May 1978)

1967-1972: Assistant Professor of History, University of Southern Michigan
Taught variety of courses in modern European history
Extensive departmental administrative responsibilities, including coordina-
   tion of counseling program

OTHER WORK EXPERIENCE

Sports writer for Dallas Times Herald, text researcher for Screen Gems
   documentary on Truman Administration, speechwriter/researcher in public
   relations firm, copyboy for NBC News

BIOGRAPHICAL DATA

Born December 31, 1940, in Dallas, Texas
Attended public schools in Duncanville (Texas) and Dallas
1958-62, Southern Methodist University (B.A.)
1962-65, Columbia University (M.A., Ph.D.)
Numerous academic honors and awards, including Phi Beta Kappa and
   Woodrow Wilson Fellowship
Fluent in Spanish
Single

*Business executive, principal, public
administrator, school administrator*

URBAN PLANNER

Evan Sims
7400 Lake Shore Drive
Round Lake, Mississippi 39663

555-1100 (office)   456-8827 (home)

CAPSULE

After ten years in publishing and public relations work, I returned to school for a master's degree in urban planning. It was my intent to combine my publishing experience with urban planning. Having now worked three years in urban planning, I am seeking a position that offers the opportunity to combine my skills with some managerial responsibilities.

WORK HISTORY

1972-present. Editor, Regional Transportation Agency. Supervise staff of two editors. Responsibilities: information gathering, writing, editing, and production on twelve annual 48-page reports published by the agency, in addition to writing and editing the annual budget report.

1968-1970. Assistant editor, social sciences, Martoni Publishing. Edited fourth-grade social-science text that was part of basal series. Purchased photography and supervised production of graphics. Worked closely with authors.

1967-1968. Junior account executive, James International Public Relations Consultants. Responsibilities: planning marketing campaigns under supervision of senior account executive; writing and production work for these campaigns.

EDUCATION

1972. Master's degree in urban planning from Round Lake University. Thesis: "The Role of Publications in Transportation Agencies."

1967. B.A. in liberal arts from Mississippi Southern State University.

REFERENCES

Furnished on request.

Junior editor, senior editor, sociologist, technical writer

4 GETTING READY TO WRITE A RESUME

This is the most important step in resume writing. It is the analytical stage, in which you consider carefully what new directions you can take or how you can put your skills and talents to their best use. It is a time to weed out those responsibilities in which you take little pleasure and to think of ways to emphasize the tasks you truly enjoy. It is also a time to gather enough basic material about yourself so that drawing on the information you have so carefully gathered, you are able to write any number of resumes slanted to various job possibilities.

Job hunting is a turning point in your life, regardless of whether or not you are doing it voluntarily, and this is the stage of resume writing where you take into account who you are and where you hope to go.

The first step in the self-analysis—and preparing your resume—is the gathering of facts. Although much of this information may seem too elementary to write down, committing it to paper causes you to think about your accomplishments, as well as your strengths and weaknesses and how they will help or hinder you on any job you accept.

Such self-analysis is not pure self-indulgence. It will help you sort out the kind of job you want and the kind of job you might best avoid, either because you would not be happy doing it or because you would not do it well.

The worksheet that follows combines a mixture of questions: some will uncover basic facts about yourself; others will cause you to think about your job needs, wants, and capacities. Some of the questions in the latter part of the questionnaire will never make it to the final form of your resume. They are important, however, because they will contribute to the tone and attitude of your resume.

Think carefully before you answer these questions. Make your answers as honest as possible. This worksheet is your personal property, and no one else need ever see what you have written.

One suggestion may help you fill in this worksheet: complete the section entitled "Analyzing Your Abilities" and then put it aside for several days. Return to it later, when you bring to it the objectivity of a little distance.

All the information you will supply on these pages could obviously be written on separate sheets of paper; you may even be tempted to do so in order to avoid messing up a book. But this book is intended to function as a workbook. It is meant to be your personal work record. If you gather this material in a permanent place, you will have to go through this stage only once. In the future, updating your resume will simply be a matter of reviewing these forms and updating them.

PERSONAL AND JOB HISTORY WORKSHEET

Section A. Education Information

Fill in the name of your high school.

_____

_____

List your best subjects.

_____

_____

_____

_____

List the subjects you enjoyed least or were poorest at.

_____

_____

_____

_____

110

List the extracurricular activities you were involved in.

_____

_____

_____

Have you pursued any of these interests today? If so, describe how.

_____

_____

_____

_____

Does any part of that extracurricular work relate to your present work experience or to any position you hope to obtain? Describe how. _____

_____

List four skills that emerged during your teen-age years.

1. _____

2. _____

3. _____

4. _____

How might these be applied to any work you hope to do?

_____

_____

_____

List exact dates of high school attendance. _____

What schooling did you have after high school? Check one.

Vocational training_____

Apprenticeship_____

Junior or two-year college_____

College_____ Number of years attended_____

List the dates of your advanced schooling, giving month and year if possible. _____

_____

_____

_____

Write the names and addresses of the schools.

_____

_____

_____

What was your major? _____

What was your minor? _____

What subjects did you enjoy most? _____

_____

_____

What subjects did you enjoy least? _____

_____

_____

List any extracurricular activities you were involved in.

_____

_____

_____

What skills or talents did you use in these activities? _____

_____

How might any of these skills or talents have a bearing on any work you do today or hope to do?

_____

_____

_____

_____

Did you work summers or part-time while attending school?____
If so, describe the amount of time you spent working and the responsibilities, skills, and talents you developed through work.

_____

_____

_____

_____

Describe how these responsibilities, skills, and talents might help you in work you do or hope to do. _____

_____

_____

_____

_____

List six skills or talents that you feel have emerged during your post-education years.

1. _____

2. _____

3. _____

4. _____

5. _____

6. _____

How might these be applied to work you do or hope to do today?

_____

_____

_____

_____

List and describe any important or major honors received in high school or college (honors society, cum laude or magna cum laude, editorships, presidencies of clubs, etc.). _____

_____

_____

_____

_____

Section B.
Work History

Beginning with your most recent job, list every job you have held full-time and fill in the information requested on the forms that follow.

Company name: _____

Dates of employment: _____

Brief description of company: _____

_____

Address: _____
              (street)

_____
        (town)   (state)   (zip)

Job title when you began: _____

Job title when you left: _____

Responsibilities and projects undertaken while employed by this company (do not forget to list one-time work assignments as well as daily tasks): _____

_____

_____

_____

_____

_____

_____

What tasks or responsibilities did you most enjoy doing and why?

_____

_____

_____

_____

What tasks or responsibilities did you least enjoy doing and why?

_____

_____

_____

_____

Describe the skills you feel you most developed during this period of employment. _____

_____

_____

_____

_____

_____

Company name: _____

Dates of employment: _____

Brief description of company: _____

_____

Address: _____
　　　　　　　　(street)

_____
　　　　(town)　　　　　　　(state)　　　　　　(zip)

Job title when you began: _____

Job title when you left: _____

114

Responsibilities and projects undertaken while employed by this company (do not forget to list one-time work assignments as well as daily tasks): _____

_____

_____

_____

_____

_____

_____

What tasks or responsibilities did you most enjoy doing and why?

_____

_____

_____

_____

What tasks or responsibilities did you least enjoy doing and why?

_____

_____

_____

_____

Describe the skills you feel you most developed during this period of employment. _____

_____

_____

_____

_____

Company name: _____

Dates of employment: _____

Brief description of company: _____

_____

Address: _____
               (street)

_____
    (town)   (state)   (zip)

Job title when you began: _____

Job title when you left: _____

Responsibilities and projects undertaken while employed by this company (do not forget to list one-time work assignments as well as daily tasks): _____

_____

_____

_____

_____

_____

What tasks or responsibilities did you most enjoy doing and why?

_____

_____

_____

What tasks or responsibilities did you least enjoy doing and why?

_____

_____

_____

_____

Describe the skills you feel you most developed during this period of employment. _____

_____

_____

_____

_____

Company name: _____

Dates of employment: _____

Brief description of company: _____

_____

Address: _____
(street)

_____
(town)   (state)   (zip)

Job title when you began: _____

Job title when you left: _____

Responsibilities and projects undertaken while employed by this
company (do not forget to list one-time work assignments as well as
daily tasks): _____

_____

_____

_____

_____

_____

What tasks or responsibilities did you most enjoy doing and why?

_____

_____

_____

What tasks or responsibilities did you least enjoy doing and why?

_____

_____

_____

_____

Describe the skills you feel you most developed during this period
of employment. _____

_____

_____

_____

_____

Company name: _____

Dates of employment: _____

Brief description of company: _____

_____

Address: _____
             (street)

_____
   (town)   (state)   (zip)

Job title when you began: _____

Job title when you left: _____

Responsibilities and projects undertaken while employed by this company (do not forget to list one-time work assignments as well as daily tasks): _____

_____

_____

_____

_____

_____

What tasks or responsibilities did you most enjoy doing and why?

_____

_____

_____

_____

What tasks or responsibilities did you least enjoy doing and why?

_____

_____

_____

_____

Describe the skills you feel you most developed during this period of employment. _____

_____

_____

_____

_____

Using a scale of 1 to 5, with 1 being "not very good" and 5 being "very good to excellent," rate yourself at each skill. Do this as objectively as possible, based on what you know about yourself and what others have told you (in job reviews, for example), because it is to your advantage to weed out the tasks you do not particularly enjoy doing and to discover the kinds of work you truly enjoy. Circle the numbers and put them right above the skills you listed.

Section C. Analyzing Your Abilities

Most of the information you have filled in on these worksheets, such as your job history, education, and personal information, will be rewritten into resume format. The final lists of your strengths and weaknesses may or may not be used in the actual resume. In some occupations, for example, you do list your skills, because they are easily outlined and vital to how well you know your job. In most jobs, though, skills and talents are subtler and less easy to pin down in a word or a short phrase.

Whether or not you use this list directly on your resume, it is a very important part of your job search. You can write a strong resume only if it is very clear in your mind what you want and how you hope to obtain it. Indirectly, the lists that follow will figure in your resume because they will give you a new self-awareness that will enable you to slant your resume not only to your qualifications but to the kind of work you most enjoy doing.

Review all the information you have compiled thus far. Using this information, compile a list of your strongest skills and talents.

1. _____
2. _____
3. _____
4. _____
5. _____

Now compile a list of your weaknesses and the things you least like doing.

1. _____
2. _____
3. _____
4. _____
5. _____

Section D. Personal Information

Is there anything in your family or personal background—fluency in a language, time lived abroad, book reviews you wrote for your local newspaper—that relates to the job you hope to obtain. If so, describe it below.

_____

_____

_____

Birth date: _____

Marital status: _____

Are you willing to travel? _____

Are you willing to relocate? _____

**Section E.
References**

References are rarely listed on a resume, but they are a vital part of the information you need close at hand during your job search.

References should include former bosses or persons who have had a working relationship with you. A prospective employer is not interested in what your minister or your grocer thinks of you. He is only seeking information on your capabilities and work habits.

Before listing someone as a reference, ask permission. You need to ask permission each time you are job hunting. Someone willing to give you a recommendation in December 1968 may not be prepared to do so in December 1978. Of course, most persons asked to give references are happy to oblige, but courtesy demands that you ask them each time you are job hunting.

Never ask for a reference from someone who you suspect may give you a poor one. It is better not to have a reference from a place you worked than to have a damaging one.

Fill in the information requested on the forms that follow so that it will be readily available when someone asks for your references.

Reference Sheet   Although references should not go on your resume, you will want to have a ready record of them to use whenever necessary. This is what this form is for.

Reference 1

Name: _____

Company affiliation: _____

Title at company: _____

Address of company: _____

Telephone number of company or home phone: _____

Extension: _____

Reference 2

Name: _____

Company affiliation: _____

Title at company: _____

Address of company: _____

Telephone number of company or home phone: _____

Extension: _____

Reference 3

Name: _____

Company affiliation: _____

Title at company: _____

Address of company: _____

Telephone number of company or home phone: _____

Extension: _____

Reference 4

Name: _____

Company affiliation: _____

Title at company: _____

Address of company: _____

Telephone number of company or home phone: _____

Extension: _____

5 WRITING A RESUME

In chapter 4, you gathered the information you needed to write a resume and did some thinking about the purpose a resume will serve for you.

In this chapter, you will take the information you have gathered and use it to create one or more resumes to suit your individual needs. Before you do that, however, you need some knowledge about the writing style and language of resumes.

Consistency

Whatever style you decide on for your resume, you must be consistent. If you indent paragraphs three spaces in the work history or employment section, then you must indent all other paragraphs the same number of spaces. Consistency—a picky item, to be sure— is a sign that you have an organized, logical mind. And while someone may not look at your resume and think, "This person failed to indent consistently," several small errors such as this add up to a messy-looking resume.

Abbreviations

Spell out most words in a resume and use as few abbreviations as possible. About the only abbreviations that are acceptable are those for college degrees—B.A. (bachelor of arts), B.S. (bachelor of science), M.A. (master of arts), Ph.D. (doctor of philosophy). Jr. and Sr. are abbreviated, as are Mr., Mrs., and Ms. Uncommon degrees—a master's in architecture, for example—should be spelled out. Spell out the names of states, cities, streets, and avenues, and titles of persons.

123

Tone   One of the most difficult aspects of resume writing is mastering the tone that is most appropriate. You must avoid sounding self-important or stuffy; on the other hand, the entire point of the resume is to sell yourself, so modesty may not strike exactly the right note, either. To avoid sounding stuffy, write in plain, clear language. Rather than saying "in regard to my previous position," say "in my last position." Try to avoid such expressions as "in regard to," "in connection with," and "on or about."

The best way to avoid sounding as if you are bragging is to use specific terms and examples to back up and describe your achievements. Below are some examples of puffed language and of alternative and better ways of saying the same thing.

Too Vague
Showed excellent signs of leadership.

Performed well under stress.

Known for my energy.

Despite a pressing deadline, the report was ready to go in time to contribute to the merger decision.

(Omit this statement and any other statement referring to your stamina, and let everything you say specifically on the resume show that you have energy and stamina.)

Better—More Specific
Organized teams of ten persons each to study the problem.

Resume language is concise and goes directly to the point. You do not have a lot of space in which to express yourself, so every sentence must be well thought out.

Some resume writers add to the tone of conciseness by avoiding the use of the first person:

> Responsibilities included marketing, budgeting, and the development of a special cost-cutting unit.

While it is certainly correct to write a resume without the use of "I," there is no reason to do so, and on some occasions, the use of "I" may be necessary. It is far more important to master the skill of saying a lot in a small aount of space. The example that follows is wordy:

> In 1958, after three years of experience in the purchasing department, all of which I enjoyed immensely, I decided that the time had come to seek a greater degree of responsibility. I applied for and was granted a promotion, from assistant buyer to senior buyer, in April.

Here is a concise version of the same paragraph:

> In April 1958, promoted to full-time senior buyer.

124

Parallelism
Parallelism—making sure that the sections of the resume that are similar to one another sound alike—is important. Many persons get caught in the parallelism trap by failing to make sure that all the verb forms in a list are in the same form. Consider these two examples:

Unparallel
Math major in undergraduate school
Spent senior year in France

Parallel
Studied math in undergraduate school
Studied in France during senior year

Skills
Reading proofs
Copy editing
Management of budget
Production skills

Skills
Proofing
Copy editing
Budgeting
Production

Jargon
The word "jargon" originally referred to a meaningless kind of gibberish. Today, ironically, it refers to the inside talk or terminology of a trade or profession. Since a resume must be read by a wide range of persons—from the director of personnel who may know little or nothing of the technical aspects of the trade that he or she represents to the fifty-year-old executive who is going to hire you but feels slightly out of touch with the new terminology of his trade—jargon should be avoided. If anything, it is a rather unimpressive way of showing off.

Sounding a Positive Note
Even professional writers have to watch the tendency to write something in a negative rather than a positive way. Sometimes it shows up in a minor way, as when someone writes, "Do not fill in lines 3 and 5," rather than, "Fill in all lines except 3 and 5." Usually, though, negativism is more subtle and reflects how you feel about yourself. This is a good reason to ask a close friend to look over your resume before you put it into final form to make sure that it hits the right, upbeat tone.

Preparing the Rough Draft
Now it is time to pull the information you collected in chapter 4 and use it to prepare a rough draft of your resume. Although you presumably did the hard work of thinking about where you want to go and how to get there as you filled in the forms in chapter 4, be equally careful about filling in these forms and you will save yourself time later.

Three forms are presented: one for new graduates, one for the historical-chronological resume, and one for the skills- or achievement-oriented resume. No form for the creative resume is included because it is so highly personal, but you can develop one using either the historical-chronological or the skills-oriented format.

NEW GRADUATE

Heading: _____

▶ *List your name, a job title, or the word "resume."*

Name: _____
_____

▶ *Do not repeat your name if used in heading.*

Address: _____

▶ *Give complete information: zip code, state spelled out, apartment number, if needed.*

Phone: _____
Job objective or title: _____
_____
_____

▶ *Do not repeat job title if used in heading. Remember to use only one or two words in job title, no more than five lines for job objective.*

Personal

Birth date: _____
Marital status: _____
Any other relevant information: _____
_____

Education

Years attended or year of graduation: _____
Name of school: _____
City or town: _____

▶ *The following is optional information.*

Major areas of study or specialties: _____

_____

Extracurricular activities that emphasized skills needed on job you
want: _____

_____

Honors: _____

_____

_____

Rank in class: _____

▶ *Use only if high enough to be impressive.*

High school attended: _____

▶ *If high school was the last school you attended, do not fill in this section.*

Year of graduation or years attended: _____

Major areas of interest or activities, if relevant:

_____

_____

Extracurricular activities that emphasize job skills:

_____

Honors: _____

Class rank: _____

▶ *List activities, honors, and class rank only if high school was the school you
most recently attended.*

Work Experience

▶ *Begin with most recently held job.*

Dates employed: _____

Title: _____

Company name: _____

Note if part-time: _____

127

Responsibilities: _____

_____

▶ *Repeat this information on separate sheets of paper for all the jobs you have held. Attach to this form.*

▶ *Don't forget to include statement about references.*

References available on request.

HISTORICAL-CHRONOLOGICAL

What heading will you use? Check one.

☐ Your name

☐ Vita

☐ Curriculum vitae

☐ Resume

☐ Resume of (your name)

Name: _____

▶ *Use only if not used in heading.*

Address: _____

City: _____

State: _____

Zip code: _____

Phone or phones: _____

Job objective: _____

_____

Employment

▶ *Begin listing with most recent job.*

Dates of employment:

From   Month _____

        Year _____

To   Month _____

       Year _____

Job title: _____

Name of company: _____

Address of company: _____

▶ *The above is not optional material.*

Description of duties and responsibilities: _____

_____

_____

_____

_____

▶ *Try to pare down and write this in resume-style language. Remember to note individual projects as well as daily responsibilities. Repeat this information on separate sheets of paper until you have described all relevant jobs. Attach sheets to this form.*

Education

From   Month _____

        Year _____

To   Month _____

        Year _____

School: _____

Year graduated: _____

Degree: _____

Major areas of study: _____

▶ *Repeat this information, moving from school you must recently attended back to high school, and write it on separate sheets of paper. Attach to this form.*

Personal

Birth date: _____

Marital status: _____

Willingness to travel: _____

Willingness to relocate: _____

▶ *Circle either of the two items above if you plan to use.*

129

Optional Categories

▶ *Fill these in only if they apply to you or your career area.*

Languages (name and level of fluency): _____

_____

Publications (briefly describe your writing experiences):

_____

_____

_____

▶ *On a separate sheet, list correct bibliographical information, books first and articles second.*

Military Service

Branch: _____

Dates served: _____

Rank of discharge: _____

Any special training or skills: _____

_____

_____

Volunteer Work

Name of group: _____

Position or title: _____

Number of years involved: From _____ to _____

Describe, as much as possible in terms that relate to business, your

responsibilities and achievements in the group: _____

_____

_____

_____

_____

▶ *Repeat this information on separate sheets of paper until you have noted all relevant volunteer work. Remember to list unofficial work, i.e., running garage sales, benefits, etc. Attach to this form.*

Skills List

If you have a set of specific skills (office or publishing production skills, for example), list them below. Then rewrite the list separately, making sure that all the items are parallel.

1. _____
2. _____
3. _____
4. _____
5. _____
6. _____

▶ *Do not use numbers in the final skills list.*

SKILLS- OR ACHIEVEMENT-ORIENTED

What heading will you use? Check one.

☐ Your name
☐ Vita
☐ Curriculum vitae
☐ Resume
☐ Resume of (your name)

Name: _____

▶ *Use only if not used in heading.*

Address: _____
City: _____
State: _____
Zip code: _____
Phone or phones: _____
Job objective: _____
_____
_____

Summary or capsule of your experience: _____
_____
_____
_____

▶ *Divide the capsule into areas of involvement or expertise. Write in paragraph form, using the first person. This section should be written almost in letter form. Use paragraphs if necessary.*

131

Employment History

▶ **Begin with most recently held job.**

From   Month _____
            Year _____

To   Month _____
            Year _____

Job title: _____

Name of company: _____

▶ **Repeat this information on separate sheets of paper until you have described all relevant jobs. Attach sheets to this form.**

Personal

Birth date: _____

Marital status: _____

Willingness to travel

Willingness to relocate

▶ **Circle either of the two items above if you plan to use.**

Education

Degree: _____

School: _____

Year graduated: _____

Major areas of study: _____

▶ **Repeat this information, moving from the school you most recently attended back to high school, or your B.A. if you have advanced degrees, and write it on separate sheets of paper. Attach to this form.**

▶ **For optional categories, turn to HISTORICAL-CHRONOLOGICAL resume form and fill in information in the categories you require.**

Once you have completed whichever of these forms applies to you, the task of transferring this information to rough, type- or hand-written form should be relatively easy. In fact, you should have to do only minor editing of what you have written on the forms.

You now have your resume in hand. All you have to do is have it typed in final form and reproduced.

Before having your resume typed in final form, use the following list to make sure that you have included all the important items of information.

- ☐ Heading (Resume, your name, job title)
- ☐ Name
- ☐ Address and apartment number
- ☐ City or town
- ☐ State
- ☐ Zip code
- ☐ Telephone numbers
- ☐ Work history
    - ☐ Correct dates of employment
    - ☐ Names of companies
    - ☐ Titles you held
- ☐ Education
    - ☐ Names of schools
    - ☐ Dates of graduation or years attended
    - ☐ Degrees awarded
- ☐ Personal information
    - ☐ Birth date (not age)
    - ☐ Marital status
    - ☐ Willingness to relocate
    - ☐ Willingness to travel
    - ☐ Any other information you plan to include
- ☐ Military service
    - ☐ Dates served
    - ☐ Rank on discharge
    - ☐ Special training
    - ☐ Special duties
- ☐ Languages
- ☐ Publications
- ☐ Professional memberships
- ☐ Statement about references, samples, or portfolio

6 OVER FORTY—AND JOB HUNTING

Looking for work after you are forty is not as easy as it is before forty. This is not to say that the older job hunter is less qualified than someone younger; indeed, the opposite is often true, for it is the older job seeker who brings experience and a high level of skill plus seasoned talents to a job. In many fields, unfortunately, prejudice does exist against the older job seeker. If you are among this group, you must learn to make some compensations for your age.

Writing your resume is the logical place to begin.

How Not to Mention Your Age

The most obvious question for any over-forty job seeker is, Do I put my age on my resume? And the answer is no, with no exceptions. It works against you if you are very young as much as it does if you are beyond a certain age. Just as you would leave out your school grade average if it did not work to your benefit, so you omit your age or any other factor that might conceivably work against you.

If you are qualified for a job, slant your resume so that this is what a prospective employer picks up first. It will most likely get you an interview. During the interview, a prospective employer can easily observe your age, but with any luck, he or she will already be so impressed with you that it will become a minor factor.

You can avoid mentioning your age by leaving out the personal section of the resume, or you can keep the information very simple, writing something such as:

Married

Will travel

Will relocate

135

Emphasizing Your Achievements

The second step in downplaying your age is to write a skills- or achievement-oriented resume, one that puts emphasis on what you have done rather than where you have worked. The chronology of your work life, while it must be included in an achievement-oriented resume, can be secondary to your accomplishments. The fact that you worked somewhere, however prestigious, is not nearly so important as what you did while you were there.

Job Objectives and Capsule Histories

A job objective (rather than a simple job title) and a capsule history are two devices that work well for the over-forty person. They are more definitive; they are more explanatory in tone than simply opening a resume with a job title. A capsule history might read as follows:

> Creative personnel manager with extensive knowledge of the field. Proficient in manpower planning, executive recruiting, EEO/Affirmative Action, benefit and pension management, and labor relations.

Be as specific as possible in a capsule history. Include the highlights of your career that you hope to capitalize on most in your next job. If you are slanting a resume toward a specific job, the capsule history should contain the achievements that will be most impressive in terms of that job.

A capsule history for a teacher might read:

> Specialist in reading education. Have developed reading-skills cards for use in grades 6 through 9 that are under/consideration for publication by major publisher in educational field. Have published five articles on reading education in major journals.

If by some fluke you happen to be fortunate enough to be over forty with only ten or so years of experience, because of extended education or military service, by all means make this work for you. You'll appear younger if you write in your capsule history, "I have ten years' experience in merchandising."

OVER FORTY, EMPLOYED, AND LOOKING FOR WORK

A decade ago, a person hoped to be fairly well settled into a job by the age of forty. Today many persons find themselves looking for work at forty and older. The new retirement age, coupled with increasing mobility in all professions and a growing sense that you do not owe your life to the company store, has led many persons to think of their careers as a series of interesting jobs rather than a settling in for life. Even major corporations reflect this attitude;

while they used to groom several young executives for the possibility of one day taking over the presidency and other top slots, many firms now hire their top management from the outside, frequently even rehiring someone who worked for them and then left to go to another company.

If you are over forty and employed, you hold a few more trump cards than an unemployed colleague does. You still, however, need to give careful consideration to the wording of your resume. Do not mention your age or birth date. Play up your experience and expertise, as well as your willingness and ability to take calculated risks. While getting a job past the age of forty becomes easier every year, don't assume that you will never have a problem related to your age simply because you still have a job. Consider carefully how your age and experience work for you, and convey this information on your resume and in interviews.

OVER FORTY, UNEMPLOYED, AND LOOKING FOR WORK

It is more difficult to psych yourself to write yet another resume when you are down over having lost your job. And with the depression that usually accompanies job loss comes a tendency to understate your achievements—something you need to avoid doing at all costs. This is hardly the time to give short shrift to your abilities, talents, and accomplishments. One way to counteract this tendency is to give yourself a little extra time—write a rough draft, put it away, and then go back to it several days later. Usually if you have been unduly hard on yourself, you will be able to spot it. This is a time to rely on the advice of others, who will be likely to spot any negative undertones in your resume more quickly than you will.

Your frame of mind has a lot to do with your success in finding a new job. Over-forty job seekers have more interesting things to say about themselves than do younger workers, and you should take whatever time you need to put yourself in an optimistic frame of mind before you actually write your resume.

Think over your achievements carefully and take full measure of your role in various companies. One advantage of age is that you can expand the role you played and be more believable than a younger worker can. You can also list more specific and major achievements. Did you save the company money? How much exactly did you save? This is a time to talk and write specific dollar amounts. Did you make money for the company? How much, and how did you do it? Was the company reorganized because of your efforts? Did any mergers or acquisitions occur in which you played an important role? These are all worthwhile achievements that should be played up in a resume; few young persons can take credit for such accomplishments.

137

Forty Plus, a club whose sole purpose is to help unemployed executives over forty find work, has noted that on first coming to their offices, many persons feel so dejected that they come up with only about 10 percent of their achievements on the resumes they write. Fortunately, the club has a policy of sending these persons back to the writing desk. It has found that just digging up and writing down in rough form what one has achieved over a twenty-year work life usually takes three to five days. If you are over forty, you would do well to spend the extra time on yourself. Now, if ever, is the time to prepare a complete and well-thought-out resume. Take four or five days to process all the information that may be relevant. There is another benefit to spending extra time on your resume when you are an over-forty job seeker. Because your experience has been more varied, you can open up a wider range of possible jobs based on your skills. More than likely, you will need several resumes. Many over-forty persons report writing one or two basic resumes and then preparing individual spin-offs as job opportunities arise.

OVER FORTY AND CHANGING CAREERS

Older job seekers will want to keep the door open to career change. Rarely are career changes drastic switches to another field; rather, they usually involve taking a job in a totally new area of their field. For example, a wide variety of jobs are open to accountants. Many persons develop an accounting specialty simply because they get a job in one area, are satisfied with it, and continue to stay in it. Rarely does specialization exclude the possibility of applying one set of skills to a new area. If you have done retail-store accounting for fifteen years, you can probably apply your skills to bank accounting, if you choose to do so.

If you are aiming toward a new career area, slant your resume in the direction you hope to go. Do not, however, write anything that suggests you are making a career switch. Simply emphasize the skills you have and how they could be applied to the new area.

Outside Activities

Sometimes over-forty workers have a tendency to emphasize professional or community achievements or even a serious avocation on a resume. You may have gotten praise for your efforts on behalf of the Boy Scouts on your last job, but resist the urge to mention it on your resume. It may only convince a prospective employer that you have outside interests too numerous or too strong for you to devote yourself to his work.

When age is working against you, you simply do not want to risk giving anyone any additional reason not to hire you.

Age as an Asset   Finally, in preparing your resume, try to think of your age as an asset. You will have to do so in interviews, and if you can reflect the same attitude in your resume—namely, that with your age come seasoned expertise and a willingness to take chances tempered with a lot of wisdom—you are already a step ahead of the crowd in the job-hunting game.

SPECIAL RESUMES FOR JOB SEEKERS

With resumes, as with almost anything else in life, practice helps build self-confidence. The more resumes you write, the better you become at writing them. And the hardest resume to write is the first one, when you are just starting out. Persons with special problems to iron out the first time they write a resume include new graduates, the foreign-born, women returning to work for the first time after rearing a family or being a housewife, and veterans who went directly from school into the service.

If you are one of these persons, the first thing you must do is gear your resume to what you have been doing. If you are a housewife who has not worked for fifteen years or a new U.S. resident, you simply cannot hide these facts nor should you want to. You should, instead, learn to write a resume that reflects your special talents and abilities.

NEW GRADUATES

All too often the new graduate writes a lengthy resume designed to cover up the fact that is most obvious to any would-be employer: This person has had little or no actual work experience.

On the other hand, as a new graduate you do have some strengths to build on, some selling points. Use the forms in chapter 4 to figure out exactly where your strengths and weaknesses lie, what it is you hope to do with your career, and then write these goals into your resume. Resist the impulse to discourse at length about where you hope to be in ten years. If it is suitable for the job you are seeking, use a job objective to describe briefly the position you hope to obtain. If you already know what kind of job you want—a junior position in publishing or a management-trainee position in banking, for example—simply use a job title.

Immediately after graduation, when you are looking for your first full-time job, is the one time you can list your academic and extracurricular honors in some detail. If you were an officer in an organization or editor of the school newspaper, note this on your resume, particularly if your activity ties in with the kind of work you plan to do.

Since there is so much competition when all the college or high school graduates hit the streets at the same time, a mass mailing of your resume may be the perfect way to get started. A mass mailing must be large; since you can expect only a 1 to 2 percent response, you must send at least a hundred resumes to get much of a response at all. Sending lots of resumes is one way for a new graduate to get started with some interviews and contacts.

Carefully read chapters 2 and 10 on format and finishing touches. Many new graduates are unaware of how to reproduce a resume or the type of paper it should be printed on, for example, and these chapters give this information.

Although printed stationery is usually recommended for anyone looking for a job, it may be inappropriate for a new graduate whose address may change in the middle of the job search. If you don't want to print an address and telephone number on stationery that may be outdated, and if using your parents' address would be inconvenient, then settle on a nice, plain, unprinted stationery and have your resume printed on the same kind of paper.

Remember, though, that a prospective employer must have some means of getting in touch with you, so put an address and phone number on your resume. If you will be moving, have only a few resumes reproduced, and then, as soon as you know your new address and phone number, rewrite the resume. If you are having only a few resumes reproduced (under fifty, for example), have copies made rather than have them printed. Professional printing is practical and economical only in large quantities, usually of a hundred or more.

Play up any part-time or volunteer work you have done on your resume. It shows your willingness to assume responsibility.

A new graduate's resume should never run more than one page— you simply don't have that much to tell yet. If you find yourself spinning out a two-page resume, go back and edit it down to one.

Keep the format simple and dignified. Creative resumes are not for the new graduate.

References may need to be handled in a special way since you cannot use ex-employers unless you have them. By all means, if you have worked part-time, try to arrange for your former employer to give you a reference. Other references that are acceptable for new graduates are those from teachers and family friends, preferably those in business. Most of the time, references will not be a problem, since prospective employers will not expect work references from a new graduate.

FOREIGN-BORN PERSONS

If you are foreign-born and fluent in another language, it will probably work to your advantage, and this skill should be noted in your resume. An employer who may not think about hiring someone bilingual may suddenly see the advantage when such a resume comes across his desk.

If you were educated and worked in another country, describe your background just as you would if you had grown up in the U.S. Mention your proficiency in languages either in the personal-information section of your resume or under a separate section for languages. If you are applying for a job in which you know your language skill would be an asset, by all means give it extra play by putting it in a separate section.

Since many countries have educational systems that differ from that of the U.S., you may want to consider adding a key word or two to clarify the level of your education. After the notation of the school that was the equivalent of high school, for example, you might write:

(Equivalent to U.S. high school)

If you have not worked for several years because of political reasons, you will need to note this on the resume in the personal-information section rather than leave a large number of years unaccounted for. There is probably no reason to explain on the resume why you left a country; if a prospective employer is interested, he will ask when he interviews you.

MINORITY GROUPS

Most companies today are keenly aware of their responsibilities to use fair hiring practices, so there is little reason to mention race on your resume.

If you do want your race noted, list organizations you belong to that are related to race rather than state your race directly.

VETERANS

The primary reason that your status as a veteran will come up on your resume is that you need to account for several years of your life. Also, some employers will give a slight edge or some advantages to veterans.

143

Military service should be listed as a separate category on your resume. Include the branch in which you served, the years served, your rank on discharge, and any special training or work that you did in the service, especially if it might apply to the kind of work you hope to obtain.

RETURNING-TO-WORK HOUSEWIVES

One advantage to being a returning housewife today is that there are more of you now than there ever have been. While the competition may be fiercer because of this, the woman who wants to return to work after rearing a family has become a familiar commodity in the job market. Employers have come to expect resumes from women returning to the work force after an absence of several years.

You will, of course, need a resume. And you will need to account for the time you spent as a housewife.

Think back over what you have done during these years—community organizations to which you have belonged, offices you have held in those groups, special interests you have had or business ventures you have undertaken. Have you organized garage sales? If so, draw up a list of the business skills you used doing this. Have you worked in political campaigns? Draw up a list of the skills and responsibilities you used doing this. Did you tutor children or do typing at home or do anything that could be described as maintaining your work skills? Did you take any courses? Write descriptions of any activities like these. Try to describe them in businesslike terms. Don't, for example, merely state that you sponsored garage sales; instead, tell how you handled the money and invoicing, the profits you earned, the organizational skills involved or the advertising.

A woman who has been out of the work world for several years should list past work experience. Give the dates you worked, the names of the employers, your titles, and describe the work you did. List any special skills you have—shorthand, typing, bookkeeping—any office machines you know how to operate.

References can be a problem if you have been out of the work force for a while. If you have done volunteer or political work of any kind, ask persons with whom you worked to give you a reference.

A chronological-historical resume works best for most returning housewives. But if you have put in a great deal of time doing volunteer work, you ought to consider writing a skills- or achievement-oriented resume.

Some employers are unduly concerned about hiring women who have children still living at home, so you may want to point out any child-care arrangements you have made or the fact that your children are now grown enough not to require full-time mothering.

Such information should be noted in a cover letter, however, not in the resume.

The most important thing for a returning housewife to remember when writing a resume is to translate any skills developed over the years to their equivalents in the business world and to make volunteer and community work experiences sound important, as indeed they are.

8

THE HANDICAPPED WORKER

Being physically handicapped can pose problems for job seekers, in the same way that being over forty or returning to work after a ten-year layoff to rear children can. It is a sensitive situation that needs to be handled in various ways, depending upon your skills, education, the prospective employer's attitude, and how you feel about yourself.

If your handicap is minor and does not interfere with your ability to work, there is probably no reason to mention it at all.

If your handicap is major, the decision to mention it to a prospective employer should be made on an individual basis. One young woman who was in a wheelchair and had developed a career in educational counseling felt that her handicap had little or nothing to do with her work capacities. While living and working in New Jersey, she applied for a job in Ohio—without mentioning her handicap in either a cover letter or resume. She was invited to an interview for the job. At this point, she considered mentioning her handicap rather than making the trip all the way to Ohio only to be disqualified on sight because of her handicap. Instead, she opted to make no mention of it and to let the fact that she had successfully managed the trip to the university speak for itself. It did, and she got the job.

On the other hand, there are definite times to mention a handicap. If you are not sure whether you can do a certain kind of work because of your handicap, it is probably better to discuss any anticipated difficulties right away. If you are in a wheelchair, for example, and you suspect that the building of a would-be employer is not wheelchair accessible, you may want to mention this to the employer in a cover letter.

Sometimes it is better to mention a handicap and describe how you function with it. If you cannot drive, for example, but have made arrangements for transportation to and from a relatively isolated place of work, you might want to include this in a cover letter.

Another time to mention a handicap is when you are applying for work with an employer who has a reputation for hiring handicapped persons. Usually you will be aware in advance of who these employers are.

Once you have decided to mention your handicap, the place to do so is in your cover letter, not in your resume. Your resume is a record of your work history and your education, just that and nothing more. Just as you would not put certain kinds of personal information about yourself in a resume, so you would not mention a handicap in one.

Do not mention a handicap at the very beginning of a cover letter. First, tell why you want the job and why you feel you are qualified; then briefly mention your handicap and any facts related to how you would handle it at work.

On page 149 is one example of a cover letter for a handicapped person, and another one is in chapter 9 on cover letters.

Dear Sir:

This letter is in reply to your ad in the <u>New Falls Times</u> of Sunday, October 13.

I have long been aware of the reputation of M-Plus Electronics and Transistors, Inc., and your leadership in the field of transistors, my specialty.

I am a graduate of the New Falls Technical School, and I am currently working on a master's in electronics science.

I should also mention that I am a paraplegic and am confined to a wheelchair. This has posed no problems for me in the three positions I have held with major electronics corporations. I have made special arrangements for transportation, and am familiar enough with the M-Plus Electronics and Transistors plant to know that it is wheelchair accessible.

I hope it will be possible for us to meet to discuss the position you currently have open. I shall call your office early next week to discuss setting up an interview.

Cordially,

Jim Smith

Jim Smith

Cover letter for handicapped person

9

THE COVER LETTER

A personnel consultant hired to help a middle-sized manufacturing company find a new president ran an ad in *The Wall Street Journal* asking for applications for the position. He received approximately 175 replies. Of these, about half were obviously from persons who were answering any ad that came along. Their resumes were general in tone, and their cover letters might have been sent to any U.S. manufacturing company.

Only six applicants stood out. They did so because their resumes were accompanied by outstanding cover letters in which each person outlined why he believed he was the person the company was seeking. The letters, the consultant reported, made him turn to the resumes attached to them. The cover letters, however, were what first caught his eye, introduced him to the applicants, and heightened the importance of the resumes that accompanied them.

Cover letters are at least as important as the resume you write, and with few exceptions, every resume should be sent with a cover letter.

A cover letter has two formal purposes: it introduces you or announces your resume, and it gets you an interview. While the resume sells you and describes what you have done professionally, only the cover letter actually asks for an interview. And any good salesperson knows that if you don't make the move to close the sale, you are likely to lose it. While getting an interview is hardly the final step in getting a job, failing to ask for an interview in a cover letter may well be the *only* reason you do not get one.

The Tone of the Cover Letter

The cover letter must grab the reader and make him or her want to read your resume. This is why a cover letter should highlight the most important items in your resume or the achievements that you think will most impress the reader.

150

A cover letter should always be as personal as you can make it. If possible, get the name and title of the person to whom you are writing. One simple way to do this is to call the company and ask for the name of the vice president of operations or the comptroller or whoever will have ultimate responsibility for hiring you. Sourcebooks like those Dun & Bradstreet publishes are also helpful in locating names and addresses.

Even if you have slanted your resume to a particular company, it must still follow the prescribed format and should include only certain items of information. A cover letter, on the other hand, can—and should—slip in that achievement of which you are extraordinarily proud or emphasize how you have saved the company money or how you have reorganized departments you have been responsible for.

A cover letter should tell the recipient exactly what he or she wants to hear. If a company is looking for a salesperson who has increased sales in other firms, and you feel that your major strength lies in introducing new sales lines, you should explain how you increased sales for your firm. The cover letter is probably not the place to bring up other achievements, once you know what the recipient of the letter is looking for. Don't dilute your sales strength.

How a Cover Letter Should Look

Try to have your own stationery printed for use in cover letters. It should be 8½ by 11 inches. White is always a safe color, although buff, light brown, manila and pale gray are also acceptable. Using a color for your stationery can pose a problem if your resume is printed on white, as most resumes are. Resumes on colored paper are not as acceptable as colored stationery, and the white paper of your resume beside your stationery may not look too good. When purchasing stationery, give thought to how it will coordinate with your resume.

Stationery should be a high-quality bond, with your vital mailing statistics printed or engraved on it. Above all, keep it simple, avoiding such typographical devices as lines or rules, cute drawings and small symbols. Printed information should include your name, address, city, state, town and zip, as well as a telephone number. This may be centered or set flush left or right, whatever pleases your eye. Your stationer can advise you about format. Stick to a plain typeface. Order matching envelopes, printed with the same information minus your phone number.

Costs of stationery vary widely, as does quality, so if money is a consideration, shop around until you find someone who meets your price range and your standards for quality.

Keeping a Record of Cover Letters

As you mail cover letters and resumes to prospective employers, keep a written record of the transaction as well as carbon copies of the letters. After an appropriate amount of time, call for an appointment. If you are turned down, consider writing a thank-you note just as you would if you had been granted an interview. (Thank-you notes are discussed in greater detail in chapter 10.)

A written record of your correspondence might look like this:

Company	Date sent	Interview	Thank-you note sent	Follow-up comments
ABC	8/5/79	8/20/79	8/21/79	No job now; opening expected mid-Sept.
LMP	8/5/79	None	8/17/79	Check back late Sept.
XYZ	8/5/79	8/23/79	8/23/79	They will call

Format of the Cover Letter

The cover letter and the thank-you note should be written in the standard format of a business letter. The parts of the business letter are shown on page 153.

Between the air of informality that pervades business today and the voices of feminism, knowing how to address someone can be a major problem. Ideally, of course, you would have the name and title of the person to whom you are writing and could therefore avoid entirely the somewhat awkward use of "Dear Sir or Ma'am." If this is not possible, you may stick to the more old-fashioned "Sir" or you may write "Dear Sir or Ma'am."

Which of the current titles to use for a woman—Ms., Miss, or Mrs.—is a personal decision unless you have some way of determining what the receiver would like to read. Ms. has become acceptable in most urban areas of the country; it is slightly less so in smaller communities and rural areas.

If you have not met the person to whom you are writing, you are probably taking too great a risk in using a first name in the greeting. Someone you know and call by his or her first name would be addressed that way in the greeting, although you should spell the name in full in the inside address.

The heading will probably be centered if you have had stationery printed; otherwise, type it flush right. On printed stationery, you can type the date under your printed heading if it looks satisfactory, or you can type it several lines below and flush right.

The inside address must be as complete as possible. Do not abbreviate anything on the inside heading, except what is shown in the example. If a line is too long to look right going across the page, type it in two lines and indent the second line, as shown in the example:

HEADING   Kevin Greene
                                                 587 Tremont Street
                                                 Indianapolis, Indiana 49744
                                                 September 12, 19__

INSIDE Mr. William Jamison
ADDRESS Mutual Life Insurance Company
           690 Meridian Lane
           Indianapolis, Indiana 49744

GREETING Dear Mr. Jamison:

BODY OF Thank you very much for meeting with me last Thursday. I was
LETTER very impressed to learn about your training program, as I had
           been told I would be by Bob Jones. I hope you will keep me
           in mind for any future openings.

CLOSE Sincerely,

SIGNATURE *Kevin Greene*

TYPED NAME Kevin Greene

Mr. Jack Roth, Jr.
Assistant to the Vice President
   of Operations
First Federal Savings & Loan
1900 Main Street
Columbus, Idaho 00000

Leave fairly wide margins and a generous amount of space at the top and bottom of the page. Since neither a cover letter nor a thank-you note should run longer than one page, try to center the letter so that it looks nice on the page. A business letter must be typed. Handwritten letters are never acceptable, nor are letters that do not pretty much follow the format just described.

Close the letter with something simple; "Sincerely" or "Cordially" will do. You should leave three or four spaces in which to sign your name, and then type your name below that. Always type your full name, even if you plan to sign only your first name. Do not type a title under your name. Even if you are employed at the time, you are not writing this letter in behalf of the company, so there is no reason to use your title.

The same advice, by the way, applies to using a company's stationery for your job- hunting activities. It not only looks bad, but could cause a future employer to wonder what you might pilfer from him.

What to Say in a Cover Letter

Keep a cover letter brief; it should rarely run more than one page. Only if the person to whom the letter is sent is well-known to you should you go into lengthy detail about how you could handle the job or save his or her company money. Unsolicited advice—and sometimes even solicited advice—is more often than not unwelcome in business.

In fact, only if you have been invited very seriously to comment about a company should you launch into a discourse on how to improve the company. Too many ill-advised persons use this attention-getting device in their cover letters only to discover too late that it gets the wrong kind of attention.

A cover letter to someone you do not know—when you are answering a blind ad, for instance—should highlight one or two of your achievements. Most cover letters consist of four paragraphs, in which you do the following—

1. State that you would like to work for the company, making sure to mention the company by name.
2. Tell why you want to work for the company.
3. Describe the qualifications you would bring to them.
4. Request an interview with them.

In paragraph 2, you aim to catch the reader's interest. You can say you have been watching his product for a while and are impressed

154

with how it is marketed, or that you want to learn a certain skill and feel that this company would be the best place to do so, or that you want to develop a specialty further and feel that XYZ, Inc., is the place to do so. Be frank and slightly forward, but do not gush.

In paragraph 3, give only two or three reasons that you are qualified to work for the company. If at all possible, make sure they are qualifications the company is seeking. Save the other reasons and lengthy explanations for your resume.

In paragraph 4, say that you are free for an interview. Persons looking for a first job or others with little experience can get away with suggesting an appropriate interview time: "I do not have classes on Fridays and wonder if I might arrange to talk with you then," or "I shall be in New York next Wednesday and Thursday, and hope we might set up an appointment on one of those days." Once you have held a few jobs and are going for a higher-level job, this ploy no longer is acceptable, and more subtlety is called for. You should definitely suggest an interview, but the time and place are best left to the person who will be seeing you.

The exception to this is when you are job hunting in one community and you live in another; then you can suggest certain days when you will be available for interviewing.

After a week and a half to ten days, plan to follow up a cover letter and a resume with a phone call, in which you attempt to firm up the appointment time and place.

Answering Blind Ads

Responding to a blind ad, one in which no company identification is offered, is a disheartening experience at best. It is particularly difficult on lower-level jobs advertised in daily newspapers; these ads often generate hundreds of responses, and more often than not, you will never get any answer to your resume and letter. Blind ads in business newspapers such as *The Wall Street Journal* or in professional journals are a different matter. Often the company is not identified because it feels the need to be confidential—and often you can figure out what the company is or at least make some assumptions about it from what the ad says.

The most awkward aspect of answering a blind ad is the greeting. Impersonal as it may seem, you have little choice but to direct the letter to the box number or whatever other address is given. The heading should probably read: "Dear Sir" or "Dear Sir or Ma'am."

Keep a careful record of any ads you respond to, plus a copy of the cover letter that accompanies your resume, because this is the only information you will have if you do receive a reply.

What you say in a cover letter written in response to a blind ad depends upon what information you are given in the ad. If you are given a lot of information about the job requirements, job experience, and type of work involved, you can respond by pointing out how your experience and training meshes with what the company seems to be seeking. On page 156 is a sample blind ad and a cover-letter response.

155

January 31, 19___
2701 Meadow Lane
Brooklyn, New York 10012

Box 210
New York Times
New York, New York 10036

Dear Sir or Ma'am:

This letter is in response to your advertisement in the Monday, January 31,
New York Times.

I believe that I may have the qualifications you are seeking. I have
worked in advertising for six years, beginning as a secretary and working
my way up to my current position as administrative assistant with a major
Madison Avenue agency. My responsibilities include preparing dossiers on
clients, product research, typing and light editing of progress reports,
and client contact, primarily by telephone. Although I am happy with my
current position, I am seeking a position that will afford me greater
opportunity for client-liaison work. Your position would seem to offer
that responsibility.

If you feel that I have the experience and skills you require, I would
very much like to meet with you personally to discuss the job. I am
enclosing a copy of my resume, which further details my work experience.
I look forward to meeting with you.

Sincerely,

Jeanne Howell

Jeanne Howell

Cover letter in response to sample
blind ad

156

If the blind ad offers very little information, then a fairly impersonal cover letter is probably the best you can do. Consider writing something like the letter on this page.

December 7, 19___
20 East Ninety-fourth Street
New York, New York 10022

Box 201
St. Louis Courier-Journal
St. Louis, Missouri 38470

Dear Sir or Ma'am:

This letter is in response to your ad of Sunday, December 3, 1978, in the St. Louis Courier-Journal. I feel that I may have many of the qualifications you are seeking, and am enclosing a copy of my resume, which describes my work experience and training in detail.

I would welcome the opportunity to meet with you personally to discuss your requirements for filling this position.

Sincerely,

Tania Oblesky

Tania Oblesky

Cover letter in response to blind ad

Content of the Cover Letter—New Graduates   If you have little or no real work experience, a cover letter will be brief, like the one on this page.

Jack Danielson, Jr.
5970 King Drive South
Chicago, Illinois 60628
September 1, 19—

Mr. Sidney Graham
Director of Personnel
CRT Manufacturing, Inc.
1900 Corporate Lane
Baltimore, Maryland 21200

Dear Mr. Graham:

I am writing to inquire about the possibility of work in CRT's personnel management training program.

My special interest in your program derives from the fact that I have spent a major part of this year working on a master's thesis about new personnel techniques developed at CRT.

I am currently completing my M.B.A. at the University of Chicago, with a specialty in personnel.

I shall be in Baltimore on September 20 and 21, and wonder if we might meet to discuss this further at that time. I shall call your office next week to see about the possibility of confirming an appointment.

Sincerely,

Jack Danielson, Jr.
Jack Danielson, Jr.

Cover letter for someone with little work experience

Content of the Cover Letter—Experienced Workers

Someone with experience would, of course, write more. Persons applying for a middle-management position might write a cover letter resembling those that begin on this page.

Jeanette Beane
450 Melrose Lane
Palo Alto, California 94303

December 15, 19__

Ms. Evelun Beckmann
Director of Cosmetics Development
Rosemont Cosmetics, Inc.
30000 Roundhill Drive
Palo Alto, California 94305

Dear Ms. Beckmann:

This letter is to inquire about the possibility of obtaining work in cosmetics development at Rosemont Cosmetics.

I presently work for a competitive firm, where I am involved in the development of skin-care creams. I am aware of Rosemont's reputation for quality in the skin-care line, and because I am most interested in pursuing this line, I am especially eager to discuss the possibility of a senior research position at Rosemont.

I have ten years of experience in cosmetology and a doctorate from the Institute of Cosmetology in biochemistry. I was largely responsible for the development of my present employer's line of skin-care products, and I have some interesting ideas for new products.

Would it be possible for us to meet to discuss this further? I shall call your office early next week to inquire about an appointment.

Sincerely,

Jeanette Beane

Jeanette Beane

Cover letter for experienced worker

Derek Mann
33 Ivy Lane
Nashville, Tennessee 37212
April 14, 19__

Talia Wedgwood
3 Potters Row
Nashville, Tennessee 37212

Dear Ms. Wedgwood:

This letter is to inquire about the possibility of joining the Potters Studio.

I am familiar with your reputation in black-on-black pottery and wish to study with you to learn more about it.

I have studied pottery under George Sienne at the Mt. Tamalpais Workshop for three years, and I currently exhibit in his shop and at the Pottery Store in Michigan.

Would it be possible for us to meet to discuss this further? My phone number is 860-1099. I shall eagerly await your answer. I shall also be happy to bring samples of my work to show you.

Sincerely,

Derek Mann
Derek Mann

Cover letter for experienced worker

George Jamison
875 North Michigan Avenue
Apartment 3007
Chicago, Illinois 60611
October 3, 19__

Mr. Donald Neely
Senior Editor
Olympia Press
50 West Forty-ninth Street
New York, New York 10020

Dear Mr. Neely:

This letter is to inquire about the possibility of an opening in the
editorial department of Olympia Press.

Your reputation for publishing quality anthropology books is known throughout publishing and in anthropology, and I have always been hopeful that one
day I might be able to combine my education in anthropology and my experience
in publishing. Olympia Press seems to offer the best opportunity for doing
that.

I have five years' experience in trade-book editing. I also have a Ph.D.
in anthropology and have done field work in Cuba on the status of women in
the sugar-cane fields, which resulted in the publication of a book by
Julian Press. I am bilingual, Spanish and English, which I mention because
I am familiar with your many fine Spanish-language books.

I would be delighted to meet with you at your convenience to discuss this
further. My phone number is 548-0900. I look forward to hearing from you.

Cordially,

George Jamison

George Jamison

Cover letter for experienced worker

Maria Sayers
40 River Drive
Princeton, New Jersey 08540
May 20, 19__

Sarton, Jones, and Sarton, Counselors
1300 Main Street
Princeton, New Jersey 18540

Dear Mr. Jones:

I am writing to inquire about the possibility of working for Sarton, Jones,
and Sarton.

I have long admired your work in tax law, and have always hoped that one
day it might be possible for me to be in a position to learn from this firm.

After earning my master's of law from New York University, I applied with
Sarton, Jones, and Sarton, only to learn that you never take on new
graduates. In the intervening six years, I have been working in the tax
department of Siliback and Siliback, and have been involved in several
major tax and antitrust cases.

Would it be possible for us to meet to discuss this further? I can be
reached by phone at 226-0400. I shall eagerly await your reply.

Sincerely,

Maria Sayers

Maria Sayers

Cover letter for experienced worker

John Boll
1400 Seneca Drive
Alexandria, Virginia 22305
March 17, 19__

Thomas McKay
Director of Operations
Computron DataProducts, Inc.
St. Louis, Missouri 63119

Dear Mr. McKay:

I am writing to inquire about any possible openings that Computron
DataProducts may have in operations.

I am especially interested in coming to work for you because for the past
two and one-half years, I have been working with your Comput 2600 system,
and I am most impressed with it. I have a strong interest in the
development of computer lines and know your reputation for quality.

I hold a B.S. in computer science and have ten years of experience in the
field. I have worked in both sales and technology. In my present
capacity as director of computer operations, I have been responsible for
introducing and setting up the Comput 2600 system.

Would it be possible to arrange a meeting so that we might further discuss
the possibility of my coming to work for you? My phone number is 282-0333.

Sincerely,

John Boll

John Boll

Cover letter for experienced worker

Gloria Skinner
4 Mountainside Drive
Littleton, Colorado 80121
February 3, 19__

Personnel Director
Sky-High Ski Lodge
40 South Mountainside Drive
Littleton, Colorado 80121

Dear Sir or Ma'am:

This letter is in reply to your recent advertisement in the Littleton
Sun-Times for an office manager.

As you can see from my resume (enclosed), I had seven years of secretarial
experience with the Maryton Hotel Chain prior to my stopping work to rear
my family.

Although I have stayed home the past five years, I have kept my hand in
the business world by doing typing in my home for small businesses and
lawyers. I type 70 w.p.m. I particularly enjoy small offices where I can
assume a greater variety of responsibilities than in a larger office. You
mentioned needing someone to run a small office, and I feel that I have the
energy and skills to do so.

Would it be possible to set up a time to talk further about the possibility
of my coming to work for you? I can be reached by phone at 982-1240.

Sincerely,

Gloria Skinner

Gloria Skinner

*Cover letter for woman returning to
work*

William Rockwell
130 Main Street East
DeKalb, Illinois 60115
June 3, 19___

Mr. John Rossner, President
Rossner Piano Manufacturers, Inc.
4500 River Road
DeKalb, Illinois 60115

Dear Mr. Rossner:

I am writing to you to inquire about the possibility of becoming a piano
tuner for Rossner Piano Manufacturers.

I have long been familiar with Rossner's reputation for making fine pianos,
and it was on a Rossner in my parents' home that I first began to play. I
now own my own Rossner.

I feel that I should mention to you that I am blind, although this has
never posed a problem in my work as an apprentice piano tuner, which I
just completed at the DeKalb School for the Blind. Although I do not
drive, I have made arrangements for my transportation to and from work,
and getting to the Rossner plant would not be difficult for me.

Could we meet sometime next week to discuss the possibility of my working
for Rossner? I shall call your office in a few days to see if we can
arrange a mutually convenient time. My phone number is 332-1776.

Cordially,

William Rockwell
William Rockwell

Cover letter for handicapped person

Cover letters require time and thought. While a cover letter will rarely take as much time to prepare as a resume will, it can hardly be dashed off. Do not become frustrated if you find yourself spending the better part of a morning on a single letter. It is important enough to be worth the time.

10 FINISHING TOUCHES

At last your resume is typed and ready to go. You have done as much work on it as you possibly can, and you feel that you have given it your best effort. It is ready to be reproduced and mailed out to prospective employers.

Now there are just a few more things to think about. First, because your resume may be the only impression you make, it must be checked and double-checked for accuracy of facts, correct spelling, and proper grammar. There are two steps you can take to ensure that your resume is as well done in this department as possible. First, put it away for a few days and forget about it. Then take it out and read it carefully again. Often you will spot something that does not sound exactly right, or notice a misspelled word or some other detail that is not exactly correct. Second, ask a friend or someone you know is good at grammar and spelling to look it over for any errors you may have missed. It does take extra effort to correct a resume at this stage—you're probably ready to be done with it—but make the effort. For all your care, someone will probably read your resume in five minutes, if that long, and spot a glaring error that will almost surely cause it to be tossed into the wastebasket. It definitely pays to have another pair of eyes take a look at your resume. One woman who was applying for the position of bank vice-president let her nine-year-old daughter take a look at the last draft of her resume and was both delighted and dismayed when the child spotted a grammatical error.

MAKING COPIES OF YOUR RESUME

Since resumes get passed out in quantity, you will need a way to make copies of your resume. You do not have to send individually typed copies, although you may occasionally want to take such pains with a resume that you are slanting very specifically toward a job you know you want.

There are two ways to duplicate your resume: by copy machine (such as Xerox) and by offset printing. Both procedures are usually handled by the same person. Look in the Yellow Pages under "instant printers," as the people who do this work are called. If you don't see the term "instant printer," there are other advertising words that indicate the type of printer you need. They are "rush work," "same day service," "photo copy," and "fast offset printing." These may not be the exact words in the ads, but anything to this effect indicates a small printer who will be willing to handle the kind of job you have in mind. If in doubt, call and ask whether he can duplicate your resume for you.

Instant printers vary greatly in quality, so you should ask to see some samples of work before you let a printer have your job. These printers can also help you print business cards and stationery, if you need it. They can also sell you plain paper stock to match the paper they print your resume on.

Instant printers vary greatly in price, so you should shop around before you make a final decision. They offer a price break if you print in quantity—for some printers, this means more than 100 copies and for others, more than 500 copies. Ask the printer's advice before you choose a printing method. If you want only ten or twelve copies, you probably want your resume run through a duplicating machine; if you want sixty copies, it still might be cheaper to have 100 or whatever the minimum is printed by the offset or photo copy method. Offset printing always gives better quality than a duplicating machine does.

One good way to find a suitable instant printer is to ask friends for recommendations.

When you bring your resumes home from the printer, store them in a place where they will stay clean and unmessed. Each resume you send must look crisp, clean, and new.

MAILING YOUR RESUME

Fold a couple of resumes with sample sheets of stationery to see what kind of fold and what kind of envelope you will need. Never mail a resume in an envelope so small that a vertical fold is required. Sometimes a two- or three-page resume will not fit easily into a regular-size envelope. In that case, use a 7½-by-18½ or an 8-by-11 envelope. That way, you can fold the resume in half once, or you can mail it perfectly flat. Larger-size envelopes have another advantage: they stand out in the morning mail.

Always find out exactly what postage your resume and cover letter require. Don't assume they can be mailed at the going rate for a first-class letter, particularly if you are using a large envelope. Making a company you would like to work for pay extra postage to find out what you are all about will never help you get the job.

Mass Mailings   If you are going to do a mass mailing of your resume and cover letters, break the task into separate steps. This is monotonous work, so it helps to enlist the neighborhood kids' assistance, if at all possible.

First, staple the sheets of your resume together if necessary. Then fold. Then stuff envelopes. Then lick the postage. Mindless as the work is, it doesn't take much time, and mass mailings can pay off. You can expect a 1 or 2 percent response rate on one, which should help you decide whether a mass mailing is worth it for your resume.

As your supply of resumes runs low, be sure to keep a couple of copies for your records.

After Mailing Your Resume   About a week and a half to two weeks after mailing your resume, you can touch base with the person you sent it to. Call and request an appointment for an interview, mentioning in the phone conversation that you sent your resume on such-and-such a day. Sometimes someone is interested in you, but assumes that you will get in touch, so always follow up by phone on a mailed resume, if possible.

Whether or not you get an interview, a thank-you note is a nice touch.

THANK-YOU NOTES—MAKING CONTACTS

A thank-you note may seem a bit extravagant, especially if you have not managed to get your foot in the door for an interview, but part of getting a job is having contacts with prospective employers—and one way of building those contacts is to remind people just as often as possible that you exist. Every time your name crosses someone's desk, the chances increase that it will ring a bell the next time.

You may stand out in someone's memory because you were the applicant who wrote a thank-you note. And when another job opening comes along—one that is especially suited to your skills and talents—someone may just remember you a little better than the other applicants because of the one small, extra contact with you.

Samples of thank-you notes follow.

Ann Rockwell
3778 Newport Road
Albuquerque, New Mexico 87100
Phone: 833-3010
February 5, 19__

Ms. Phyllis Knight
Vice President, Personnel
Vue Limited
800 Boswell Street
Venice, Ohio 45174

Dear Ms. Knight:

I enjoyed talking with you Monday about the prospect of coming
to work at Vue. I especially appreciated hearing of Vue's
track record with women, which is outstanding. When Vue has
an opening, I hope you will have me in mind. I feel that my
qualifications and work experience would fit in well at Vue.

Again, thank you for your time.

Sincerely,

Ann Rockwell

Ann Rockwell

Julia Rossi
2700 Lake Lane
Byington, Missouri 63638
April 22, 19___

Mr. Anton Casewit
Chief Manager-Personnel Relations
Kent Manufacturing, Inc.
1200 Lake View Lane
Byington, Missouri 63638

Dear Mr. Casewit:

Thank you for taking the time to talk with me about trainee
positions at Kent. I was especially impressed with your training program, having looked at several others in the past few
months, none of which seemed to offer the wide range of
experience that Kent's does. I hope I shall be hearing from
you.

Sincerely,

Julia Rossi

Julia Rossi

                              William S. Porter
                              887 Skyline Drive
                              Waverly, Wyoming 82335
                              October 1, 19—

Mr. Richard Bertrand
ABC Manufacturing, Inc.
5000 Marvel Lane
Waverly, Wyoming 82335

Dear Dick:

I enjoyed our meeting last week and the tour of your plant yesterday. I
am quite impressed with the whole operation, and I'm finding myself in-
creasingly tempted by the possibility of coming to work for you as your
comptroller.

I was delighted to discover that our business philosophies are so similar.
I look forward to continuing our talk soon.

Cordially,

Bill Porter

William S. Porter

REVISING YOUR RESUME

If you have followed the steps listed in this book and have saved this book as your permanent resume record, revising a resume should be a relatively simple and painless task.

Resumes become outdated when some piece of personal information changes (a good reason to include as little as possible), when you lose a job, or when you decide to look for a new job.

To update your resume: Read it carefully, circling in red ink any items that are no longer accurate. On separate sheets of paper, write in substitute information blocks for the ones that need to be changed.

If some item needs to be dropped entirely, cross it out.

Some persons date resumes. If you have done this, remember to change the date.

Read over your changes to make sure they follow the style and format of your old resume. Retype your resume, adding new information as needed.

Bibliography

Numerous books have been published on changing career directions, women returning to work, and how to find a job. For more information on these, consult with your local librarian.

Harder to locate, however, and just as important for the resume writer are books on writing well and using proper grammar. Obviously, no one wants to read a grammar book prior to writing a resume, and there is some question as to how effective this would be, anyway. Instead, here is a list of books that are not ponderous and that will show you how to write correctly.

Bernstein, Theodore M. *The Careful Writer*.
New York: Atheneum, 1977. Excellent book on the use of good English.
Goeller, Carl. *Writing to Communicate*.
New York: New American Library, 1974. Good book on all kinds of business writing.
A Manual of Style. 12th ed., rev.
Chicago: University of Chicago Press, 1969. Actually the bible of authors and editors, this book is helpful to anyone who writes. Unlike the other books on this list, it is available in hardback only.
Shaw, Harry. *Punctuate It Right!*
New York: Harper & Row, 1963. A comprehensive guide to punctuation.
Strunk, William, Jr., and E.B. White. *The Elements of Style*. 3rd ed.
New York: Macmillan, 1979. A classic, this small, highly readable paperback is the best single book you can read on writing correctly. It explains everything clearly and painlessly.